SOVIET ATTITUDES TOWARD AUTHORITY

An Interdisciplinary Approach to Problems of Soviet Character

SOVIET ATTITUDES TOWARD AUTHORITY

An Interdisciplinary Approach
to
Problems of Soviet Character

Margaret Mead

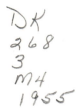
William Morrow & Company, Inc., New York, 1955

SOVIET ATTITUDES TOWARD AUTHORITY

An Interdisciplinary Approach

to

Problems of Soviet Character

Copyright; 1951

Margaret Mead

Printed in the United States of Amercia

Contents

Chapter 1

QUESTIONS WHICH THIS STUDY SEEKS TO ANSWER

A primary task of the mid-twentieth century is the increasing of understanding, understanding of our own culture and of that of other countries. On our capacity to develop new forms of such understanding may well depend the survival of our civilization, which has placed its faith in science and reason but has not yet succeeded in developing a science of human behavior which gives men a decent measure of control over their own fate. This book is a report on an interdisciplinary-group approach to the study of certain aspects of Soviet attitudes toward authority. My role as director has been to help to integrate the approaches of my colleagues within an anthropological framework and to prepare this report of the work which we did together.

The problem of forming reasonably accurate estimates of social and political conditions within the Soviet Union, of calculating directions of change, and of assaying the significance of single events presents peculiar difficulties because of the impossibility of attaining direct access to the Soviet people, because of the highly centralized ideological screen through which all public materials have to pass, and because of the strength of feeling for and against the political system of the Soviet Union which has resulted in the positive or negative coloring of almost all first-hand reports. It is these obstacles to direct observation which justify the use of the type of analysis which will be attempted in the following pages. Ideally, the anthropologist works on the spot, and, to attempt an understanding of the areas which have been covered in the background for this report, field workers would have been placed in plants and factories, in collective farms and Machine Tractor Stations, on Party committees, in the editorial rooms of journals and newspapers, in the schools, in Komsomol meetings. Not only the contents of a book or a film, but the response of the readers and of the audience would have been investigated. The proportion of the population who read a propagandistic pamphlet or followed in detail a governmental injunction would have been determined by sampling methods. Hypotheses regarding the character structure of different groups, the Party members, the skilled workers, the managerial class, etc., would have been tested by interviews and observation, by data from the clinic and the consulting room.

1

These methods cannot be applied to the present task. It has therefore seemed worth while to collect such data as were available and to analyze these *as if* one were giving an anthropological analysis of authority problems within a society which it had been possible to study by direct field methods. Such a procedure has the advantage that it uses the anthropologist's training in relating isolated items of behavior to a systematic whole, in remembering that abstractions like "The Party" or "Soviet agriculture" are convenient ways of describing certain of the institutional activities of Soviet men and women, but that the same Soviet man may be a Party member, the manager of a Machine Tractor Station, a father, a reader of a novel, a man who responds or fails to respond to a cartoon in *Krokodil,* who takes the mandates of the Party with extreme seriousness or executes them with his tongue in his cheek. If this focus on the individuals who appear and reappear in the different phases of Soviet life is maintained, then it is possible to outline certain regularities in their behavior and to trace these regularities through the organization of the Party, the way in which a collective farm functions, or the admonitions given to teachers of small children. The words which a novelist puts into the mouth of an approved heroine, or the scolding which is given in *Pravda* to collective farmers who steal grain, or the methods used to recruit skilled labor by appropriate political prosecutions can all be used as data on the behavior of the Soviet people who live within the Soviet Union.

With such data, we can attempt to answer such questions as the following: What are the patterns of behavior between those in authority and those over whom they have authority? Are these patterns of behavior congruent with the ideals of behavior which are constantly preached in the schools and in the youth organizations? When we analyze the attempt to remake the old type of Great Russian into "the new Soviet Man" through adult education, political indoctrination, new forms of organization, and the attempt to bring up children to fit the new ideals, do we find contradictions which may be sources of weakness in the present, of revolt, or of change in the future? Can we form an estimate of the type of devotion or acceptance of the Party and the State which is characteristic of the great mass of Soviet citizens who do not emigrate against which we can interpret the testimony of those who do emigrate?

If we can form hypotheses on problems such as these, they will have direct bearing on such questions as the type of loyalty which may be predicted for border populations or the sorts of pressure exerted upon a chairman of a collective farm by central authorities on the one hand and the members of the collective on the other. An informed estimate of the response of Soviet citizens at different levels to changes in the Party Line coupled with our historical knowledge of the shifts in the Line should make it possible to estimate the morale differential and resistance to propaganda of different age groups or of individuals with different status in the Party, armed services, or industry.

Americans are daily forming opinions regarding the public behavior of Soviet officials or events in the Soviet Union which hinge directly on the answers to such questions as these: What is the Soviet attitude toward compromise? What types of behavior are regarded as permissible and ethical which we would regard as impermissible and as involving those who practiced them in depths of cynicism? At what level, for what purposes, can we say that Soviet officials are sincere? How does this sincerity differ from our sincerity?

A second group of questions concerns the internal structure of the Soviet Union: the meaning of organizational changes, the extent to which different parts of the "apparatus" are rivals, the relationship between the actual clique formation and the official ideal picture which is given to the average Soviet citizen and to the world.

Many of these questions might be summarized briefly in the following manner: What is the nature of the hold which the contemporary authority system in all of its ramifications—Party doctrine, centralized organization, economic rewards and punishments, censorship, political police, and educational system—has on the population? What are the conditions under which this hold may be expected to get stronger, to remain the same, to get weaker?

It is toward answers to these questions that the following analysis is directed.

Chapter 2

METHODS AND MATERIALS

The method used in this study is one which has been developed during the last decade for the study of cultures at a distance, using individual informants and written and visual materials where field work is impossible. The anthropologist brings to this approach his training in preliterate societies, where he has had experience in the use of living informants and in tracing regularities among many disparate elements of a culture small and simple enough to grasp as a whole. While it is quite impossible ever to obtain the same grasp of the culture of a great complex literate society, and while it is always necessary to rely on the combined research and experience of many disciplines, the anthropologist's way of looking at the materials can still be used.

This particular anthropological approach goes beyond the mere identification of such regularities in different aspects of a culture. It attempts to integrate these observed patterns of behavior, as reported by historians, economists, political scientists, and other specialists, with our knowledge of the growth and development of human beings and with the findings of the psychologist and psychiatrist on the functioning of human personalities.

Probably because this method has been developed as an applied science to deal with problems of great human urgency without the protection of an ivory tower, it has been subjected to a very large amount of misrepresentation.

(1) It has been asserted that this method attempts to trace political and social institutions back to events of infancy. This is not so. Events to which the growing child is regularly subjected in any society are invoked to analyze the way in which the child learns his culture. The critic has confused here three kinds of statements about origins: (a) the origin of the particular anthropologist's insight (in the sense that a study of the way a child is taught to eat may give a clue to cultural attitudes toward scarcity or responsibility; (b) the origin, within the life span of the individual, of that *individual's* understanding or appreciation of an institution, in the sense that a child's religious view of a Heavenly Father may be shaped by the behavior of its human father; and (c) statements about origins of political and social institutions. The anthropologist does not differ from other students of social institutions in his recognition that social and political institutions have long histories and have been shaped by many generations of human beings within changing social,

4

physical, and technological environments. Though the origins of all social institutions are complex and cannot be traced to any *single* cause, institutions persist by being embodied in each generation, which must learn the appropriate behavior and acquire the appropriate character structure, and changes in any society of any duration must be expressed in changes in these learnings, in which case the accompanying character structure will change also.

(2) It has been asserted that in this approach caste, class, occupational and regional differences are ignored. Where the material is available and relevant, these differences are taken into account; but this method has been used primarily to deal with behavior in national and international contexts, in which it is possible only to know the national culture from which a given newspaper or propaganda leaflet, broadcast, army, or mission comes. We may be able to identify the particular region or subculture or class which plays a dominant part in shaping some or all aspects of national policy—for example, the role of men with public-school education in traditional British foreign affairs, or of Great Russian culture in contemporary Soviet culture—but primarily we are concerned with those regularities in the behavior of citizens of a nation-state which can be attributed to the fact that such citizens were reared or have lived for a long time under the influence of a set of nationwide institutions. Knowledge that a man is a Soviet citizen does not make it possible to tell what language he speaks, what food he prefers, or to what place names he responds with nostalgia, but it does make it possible to state certain aspects of his relationship to the police system, to rationing, and to his available reading matter.

Such a statement regarding "national character" is necessarily bare and schematic, omitting the nuances of region and class and unable to do justice to the unique ways in which individual personalities express their culture. When an anthropologist describes a whole primitive culture, or a historian a whole period, the description is richer than the actual content of any individual personality, as no one person, however precise his class and regional representatives, ever embodies all the intricate detail of his culture. So where reading a full account of one's culture is felt to be ennobling, reading a schematic description of a certain set of regularities which one shares with every other national of the same country—a description which is not a composite portrait, not even a snapshot, but only a diagram—is felt to be impoverishing. When such a diagrammatic statement also includes references to parts of the character which have become unconscious—either as a child learning to reconcile its impulses with cultural demands, or as an immigrant, sternly repressing memories of the past—the resistance of the reader may be even stronger. Yet such diagrammatic statements have proved useful for special purposes: to predict the behavior of members of one culture as compared with another and to comprehend and allow for large-scale changes which are taking place in contemporary cultures.

(3) It has been asserted that anthropologists assume that the character structure of a people is static and unchangeable, which is equivalent to a form of racism. This is not so. This assertion confuses the methods used by anthropologists in dealing with primitive societies when there are no records and for which, therefore, change can only be inferred from indirect evidence and so cannot be studied systematically, with anthropologists' approach to modern societies in which they recognize rapid change and profound discontinuities between generations as being the rule. However, we also recognize that changes are made by human beings, themselves reared within the existing culture, and that the new character structure will therefore be systematically related to the old, sometimes as a deviation at only one level, sometimes as an extreme counterpoint, as a new class or a special segment of the population comes into power. The more rapid the change, as in successful revolution or when large numbers of individuals emigrate as adults, the more conspicuous are the relationships between the old and the new character. This book is an attempt to examine contemporary Bolshevik character, which may be seen either as a new, special version of old Russian character or as a new Russian character, and the institutions which Bolsheviks are developing to shape the next generation.

In this approach it is assumed that human infants begin life in every human society—of comparable size—with a comparable range of abilities and potentialities. It is assumed that differences reported by all students of human societies as existing between one culture and another—differences in language, social organization, religious belief, etc.—are in no way to be related to any racial characteristic of the members of these societies, but must be learned by each generation. It is further assumed that, while the particular form of the culture of any society—the United States, or the Soviet Union, or the Republic of Indonesia—is to be related to a long sequence of historical events within a given geographic context, the fact that a given group of adult members of a society embody an historically developed culture is to be referred to the circumstance that they either have been reared in those particular cultural forms or have emigrated and subsequently have mastered them. Because of man's common psychophysiological equipment, it is possible to explore the way in which different cultures are learned by human beings with comparable abilities and so to learn something of the cultural character of those who perpetrate a culture and participate in revolutionary or evolutionary changes which take place within that society. When changes occur, especially the drastic changes which accompany a successful revolution, it is possible to relate these changes to the existing learned behavior and to ask, How will individuals who embodied the old culture behave within the new revolutionary forms? To what classes, or personality types, or sorts of experience can we relate the insistence on new behavior and the repudiation of the old? How does a knowledge of the way in which the old culture was learned or of how the new emerging culture is acquired—when placed against a comparative knowledge of how all children and adults learn—add to our ability to understand and to predict?

Throughout such research, emphasis is laid upon combinations rather than upon single items, upon configurations of widely diffused or universal aspects of human behavior. Just as every language is made up of sounds shared with other languages, of grammatical devices shared with whole families of languages, so the patterns of learning within any culture share many single items with neighboring cultures or with cultures which derive from common historical roots. In identifying the regularities within any one character structure, the anthropologist attempts to show how the particular combination of interpersonal events by which parent and child or old resident and new immigrant communicate with each other is organized to produce a character which can be identified as American, or Russian, or French, or Greek, or Siamese.

Furthermore, this new approach has to work out relationships with other disciplines which have been the traditional ways of studying historical societies.

This approach is meant to supplement rather than to replace the findings of other disciplines by relating the mechanisms within the individual to wider descriptions of social process. The social sciences have already made outstanding contributions to our understanding of contemporary Russia by analyses in terms of such organizing abstractions as revolution, the pace of industrialization, and the characteristics of dictatorships. Such analyses can be given additional usefulness if such large-scale changes can be described in terms of what has happened and is happening to the Russian people who are participating in them. Findings from this method should not be expected to contradict any other analysis of the Soviet Union which is based on scientifically viable hypotheses, but they should reveal hitherto unidentified connections, open up further lines of research, and thus increase our capacity for prediction.

This report concentrates on the special contribution of this method without continually repeating the interpretations which other disciplines place on the same phenomena. For example, the success of the centrally controlled police state may be related by historians to earlier models in Russia or in Asia or in the Near East, and the functioning of the NKVD may be compared with that of the Janissaries; political scientists may discuss twentieth-century totalitarian models; political philosophers, the role of Marxist philosophies of power; and economists, the peculiar Soviet methods of solving problems of full employment by methods which call on the political police to provide a specified number of politically suspect skilled carpenters. This report will stress the relationship between a police system which does not seek to fix responsibility accurately for a particular crime but which operates with diffuse terroristic methods and a characteristic of Russian behavior which, by equating treasonable thoughts and treasonable acts, makes the acceptance of such a police system, both by those who execute it and those who live under it, *different* from the acceptance of such a system in another society. Where the other disciplines will invoke as explanatory concepts "Russia's peculiar historical position," "the level of industrialization," and "the Hegelian dialectic," this approach will invoke the learned behavior of Russians, particularly of Great Russians, and more particularly those Russians who became Bolsheviks, not in opposition to these other explanatory concepts, but in addition to them. The comparative anthropological approach lays stress upon differences between cultures, upon the basis of an acceptance of a common humanity, in comparable situations—such as revolution—and upon a recognition of the diffusion of ideologies, such as Communism, beyond the limits of one culture. But it is the distinctively Russian version of humanity, the distinctively Russian aspects of the Revolution, the distinctively Russian interpretations of Communism upon which the anthropologist would expect to throw additional theoretical light. When we stress these distinctively Russian characteristics, we do so in recognition that there are many formal resemblances among revolutionary situations, that Communism is found in other countries, and that totalitarian regimes have certain organizational aspects in common. These considerations have been systematically taken into account with the help of the historians and political scientists in the group. This discussion of certain aspects of Soviet attitudes toward authority thus proceeds within the context of historical and political scholarship on the Soviet Union but will limit itself to such aspects of the question as are not dealt with in this form by the other disciplines.

In an undertaking such as this it is necessary for the reader to have a record of who did the work and of how it was done.[1] We were a staff of nine with two consultants; all but two—of whom I was one—were familiar with Russian culture and the Russian language. Each research worker assumed responsibility for the selection and analysis of materials in specific areas within a framework provided by individual consultation and group seminar.

Six areas were chosen for analysis: (1) the Party, the two youth groups which prepare for the Party—Komsomols and Pioneers—and the records of the trials of the Old Bolsheviks in the late thirties (selected as a part of the most recent material on communication within the top levels of the Communist

---

[1] This project was originally suggested to RAND by Professor Ruth Benedict, who was also directing a series of researches on contemporary cultures, under a grant from the Office of Naval Research, known as Columbia University Research in Contemporary Cultures. When Professor Benedict died in September, 1948, I succeeded her as director of Columbia University Research in Contemporary Cultures and was asked to assume in addition the direction of this project, which was then reorganized as Studies in Soviet Culture under the American Museum of Natural History. Dr. Nathan Leites, a member of RAND's scientific staff, acted as research coordinator, with special reference to the political relevance of the material.

Party of the Soviet Union); (2) leadership in agriculture; (3) organizational problems of industry; (4) education, especially official standards for parental behavior and school practice; (5) contemporary literature, both adult and juvenile, especially direct and indirect expressions of disapproved attitudes and behavior; and (6) the new folklore concerning Lenin and Stalin. The published materials used—having been published within the Soviet Union—must be assumed to have been, at the time of publication, approved by the regime. They may therefore be taken as indications of what the top echelons of the CPSU would like the lower Party echelons—the worker, or the member of a collective farm, the parent or teacher—to believe and do, and of what types of thinking and acting were or are disapproved. These materials provide no direct information on the extent to which those to whom they are addressed believe what they read or on the extent to which they act upon it. This is preliminary research to construct hypotheses concerning the responses of the Soviet population to these materials and the way in which the enjoined ideals are carried out in practice.

In order to interpret further these materials, the following steps were taken: (1) Recent emigrants were interviewed. (2) The personal experience of members of the research group who had worked at various times and in various capacities within the Soviet Union or with representatives of the Soviet Union was thoroughly exploited. (3) There was a systematic inclusion of hypotheses on the character structure of different groups in pre-Soviet Great Russia, especially of peasants and intelligentsia, which had been developed in the Russian section of the Columbia University Research in Contemporary Cultures by Geoffrey Gorer.[2] These had been derived primarily from interviews with adult Great Russians, using methods of interpretation based on our present knowledge of human growth and the educational practices of a society as embodied in the character structure of adults. (4) Parallel hypotheses on the special Bolshevik version of this older Russian character structure, as developed by Dr. Nathan Leites[3] through a detailed analysis of the works of Lenin and Stalin, were included and systematized with reference to our present knowledge of the less articulate aspects of human psychology. (5) Critical use was made of comparative anthropological studies of social structure and of the relationship between certain types of social structure and certain types of character structure.[4]

[2] Geoffrey Gorer and John Rickman, *The People of Great Russia, a Psychological Study,* Cresset Press, London, 1949; Chanticleer Press, New York, 1950, 236 pp; Geoffrey Gorer, "Some Aspects of the Psychology of the People of Great Russia," *The American Slavic and East European Review,* Vol. 8, Octboer, 1949.

[3] *The Operational Code of the Politburo,* The RAND Series, McGraw-Hill Book Company, Inc., New York, 1951.

[4] M. Mead, *Cooperation and Competition in Primitive Societies,* McGraw-Hill Book Company, Inc., New York, 1937; G. Bateson, *Naven,* Cambridge University Press, London, 1936.

Within this apparatus of interpretation, selected materials were analyzed in detail by methods of tracing connections and delineating patterns which are used by anthropologists, linguists, clinical psychologists, and psychiatrists. Every effort was made to use this approach (which has been developed on a known context) against a critical historical background.

This report does not attempt to document the findings of the Studies in Soviet Culture project. Appendix D presents a detailed account of the large amount of published source materials which was systematically examined by different members of the research team who specialized in materials of a given order; for example, pedagogical literature, letters to the press on a given subject, and literary controversy, during a specified period of time. The selections which each research worker made were processed as working papers and made available to the entire research group. Each member of the group participated in developing hypotheses for further exploration of these particular materials. The choice of illustrative material used in this study was checked by the specialist who originally contributed the particular quotation. It therefore seems valid to draw illustrative materials from sources covering the whole life of the Soviet Union without in each case giving an account of how the contextual relevancy has been established. The varieties of experience in the group are the guarantee that material has been used only with full and systematic consideration of the date, the particular setting, the type of publication, and the local historical situation, etc. The problems in this report have been considered against Soviet society, seen as a whole, and against a conception of traditional Great Russian character and emerging Soviet character. These cannot be discussed in full in a report of this length, and only such aspects as fall within the range of this inquiry will be dealt with; but in the discussion of Soviet police terror, for instance, although the state of transport, record-keeping, fingerprinting, etc., will not be elaborated, it will have been taken into account.

Nor are the hypotheses suggested here meant to be complete explanations of particular events—as providing, for example, an explanation of the great purges of the late thirties, which have their very special historical context. If the hypotheses presented here are to stand up, then nothing which we know about the great purges should conflict with them, but there is no expectation that the entire course of the great purges should be derivable from them. Studies of culture provide better bases for prediction the larger the number of members of a culture involved in the prediction: they are more valid for the behavior of a group of critics than for the writer of a single work of fiction; for the response of the populace than for the writer of a single broadcast or the behavior of a particular political leader. While the behavior of the single writer, the particular editor, or the political leader must be systematically related to the culture to which each belongs, it cannot be specifically predicted from it, although the limits within which it may fall may be established.

In attempting to describe that particular version of human behavior which may be represented as being contemporary Russian, and showing how contemporary Soviet political action may be referred to such characteristics, there is no suggestion that the political behavior of the Soviet Union is solely self-generated and in no way responsive to and influenced by political events in the world outside the Soviet Union. Nevertheless, in this political situation within which the Soviet leaders are responding to internal and external events there should be considerable usefulness in discriminating the special Russian character of these political behaviors.

I have prepared this report on the basis of the materials developed by the research staff and with criticism and consultation from members of the group, especially from Geoffrey Gorer, Nathan Leites, and Philip E. Mosely. I am not only not a Russian specialist, but I do not speak Russian and I have been able to do only a minimal amount of interviewing or first-hand analysis of materials. I have had twenty-five years of experience working on comparable problems among primitive and contemporary people and several years of experience in relating researches of this sort to specific national and international problems. This book must be understood as an attempt to point up some of the implications of the work of the project team. The members of the research group are responsible for the selection of the concrete materials which have been used and for criticizing the contexts within which I have used them, but I alone am responsible for the theoretical phrasing, based as it is on the insights, research, and formulations of the members of the two Russian projects with which I have been associated.

This was a pilot project. Hypotheses which have been developed during a year and a half of systematic research await elaboration and further verification.

Research Team of Studies in Soviet Culture and Their Areas of Research

Margaret Mead, Director, anthropologist; integrating, working with, and supervising the research staff with special emphasis upon a cultural frame of reference.

Nathan Leites, political scientist; specializing in an analysis of the trials of the Old Bolsheviks; integrating, working with, and supervising the research staff with special emphasis upon political relevance. Member of the Social Science Division, The RAND Corporation.

Elena Calas, psychiatric social worker; specializing in Soviet child-training ideals and ideas of authority in Soviet children's literature.

Elsa Bernaut, Slavic linguist; specializing in analyses of the trials of the Old Bolsheviks and of conflicts within the Party.

Herbert Dinerstein, historian; specializing in studies of Party unity and organization and case studies of the way in which Party ideals of organization work out in agricultural management. Member of the Social Science Division, The RAND Corporation.

Leopold Haimson, historian; specializing in studies on Party unity and organization and case studies of the way in which Party ideals of organization work out in management of industry.

Nelly S. Hoyt, historian; specializing in analysis of Soviet youth training ideals and Communist synthetic folklore about Lenin and Stalin.

Vera Schwarz (Alexandrova), literary analyst; specializing in delineation of images of types of conformity and nonconformity in contemporary Soviet literature.

Nicolas Calas, literary analyst; working on the relationship between attitudes toward authority in the Greek Orthodox Church and contemporary Soviet attitudes.

Ralph T. Fisher, graduate student in history; making a special study of the Eleventh (1949) Congress of the Komsomol.

Consultants

Geoffrey Gorer, anthropologist; scrutinized the concepts developed in Studies in Soviet Culture in the light of the basic hypotheses concerning pre-revolutionary Great Russian character structure which he developed for the Columbia University Research in Contemporary Cultures in 1948–49.

Philip E. Mosely, historian; has provided historical orientation and criticism in the light of his experiences with contemporary Soviet political behavior.

Chapter 3

BACKGROUND OF THE SOVIET SYSTEM
OF AUTHORITY

As a background for this study, certain broad historical tendencies in pre-Soviet Russia must be taken into account. In the nineteenth century, Russia, hitherto a caste society, developed a group recruited from various castes known as the "intelligentsia," defined by education and attitude rather than by birth and without the definiteness of place in society which the old castes occupied. This group reacted strongly against many tendencies in the old Russia, such as the miserable conditions of the lower castes in country and city and the backwardness of the whole life of the country. During the decades in which members of this group came out both openly and secretly against the status quo, a rapid industrialization set in. While most of the industries were in the hands of private capital, Russian and foreign, the State played a major role in fostering industrialization through direct subsidies, guarantees of interest to investors, loans, guaranteed contracts for purchase of output, free importation of equipment, and high tariffs on competitive imports as well as through preventing the formation of trade-unions and punishing the outbreak of strikes, thus assuring to the new industries a supply of unorganized and cheap, if not always docile, labor. The new capitalist class was small in number, weak in prestige and subservient to the autocracy, and it provided little if any support for the growth of liberal and democratic demands for reform. Under these conditions, Marxist doctrines imported from the industrialized West had to be adapted to a society in which the enemy consisted of an amalgam of Tsarist bureaucrats, large landowners, foreign and domestic capitalists, etc. With no trade-union movement of a character such that labor leadership might have grown out of it, leadership became largely the task of a small group of self-dedicated intellectuals. Despite the widespread feeling of solidarity among the intelligentsia, many diverse programs developed, surrounded by furious controversy.

Lenin and the group of Bolsheviks around him had the task of shaping from a group of fervent, talkative, impractical intellectuals who had been mainly concerned with reacting *against* tyranny and exploitation rather than with the development of any practical program, a group capable of seizing power and of holding it once it was seized. At the same time, everything—institutions and persons, they themselves as much as the rest of the population—had to be remade into something different from the old.

13

Strict forms of political control, centralization of government and industry and political police who watched over a people adept at indirect forms of resistance, did not need to be invented but had merely to be shaped to new purposes. For example, under the peasant commune, or *mir*, which was the dominant form of rural life in Great Russia until 1928, the peasants were accustomed to regard the land as owned by the community or by the Tsar, not by the individual peasant, to decide on the joint planning of village work (times of planting, harvesting, stubblegrazing, etc., had to be uniform), and to perform some forms of community work together. Conscription of community labor for state needs had long been a tradition, which was gradually abandoned only after the 1860's; and, in fact, the peasants usually clung to the custom of providing free labor for this purpose in preference to paying additional taxes.

Russian Communism, using Marxist theory but grounded in Russian conditions, developed by men imbued with a Russian attitude toward life, has had a double emphasis. It fought against certain aspects of old Russia but also against certain aspects of the West seen from Russia. It opposed the sluggish apathy and the tendency of old Russia to accept fate and also opposed the romantic, despairing, or overoptimistic adventurousness of those who reacted against resignation; it turned against those who wished to go too fast as well as against those who wished to go too slowly. This double character of Russian Communism (which in future will be referred to as Bolshevism) has become familiar to the world in the picture of a struggle around a central position from which the "rights" and the "lefts" are always "deviating," with those in power always trying to overcome both deviations, sometimes by absorbing parts of one deviating group, sometimes by using one group to destroy the other, sometimes —when strong enough—by lumping rights and lefts together and destroying them both.

The use and ideology of supreme power in the Soviet Union have certain unique characteristics, in addition to the circumstances that they were developed directly following a hereditary monarchy with a highly centralized bureaucracy and that the Soviet Union is a dictatorship which shares with other dictatorships the totalitarian demand for control over every aspect of life. The very considerable tightening of controls in the Soviet Union, as compared with the Tsarist regime, may be explained in part by the fact that a traditional regime reacts to overt signs of rejection; a new regime demands active proof of loyalty.

There are also certain aspects of the Bolshevik version of Marxism which must be held in mind. One of these distinctive aspects is the theory of the Party Line. The Bolshevik concept of the Party Line sums up the doctrine that the policy-making group knows the "correct" course to take. Krupskaya, Lenin's widow, said at the 14th Party Congress in 1925:[5]

---

[5] N. Krupskaya, 14th Congress of the All-Union Communist Party (*XIV s'ezd Vsesoyuznoi Kommunisticheskoi Partii*), stenographic account, Moscow, 1926.

> For us, Marxists, truth (*istina*) is that which corresponds to reality. Vladimir Il'ich (Lenin) said: The teachings of Marx are immovable because they are true (*verno*), and our congress should concern itself with searching for and finding the correct line. It is impossible to reassure ourselves with the fact that the majority is always right. In the history of our party there were congresses where the majority was not right (*neprav*). . . . The majority should not get drunk (*napivat'sya*) with the idea that it is the majority, but should disinterestedly search for a true (*vernyi*) decision. If it will be true (*vernyi*) it will put our party on the right path.

The Line, as understood by the policy-making group, represents absolute Truth; therefore, while temporary retreat before a strong enemy may be necessary and in fact dictated by the Line itself, true compromise—in the Western sense—is not comprehensible to the Bolshevik leadership. As one American negotiator reported in an unpublished memorandum:

> During negotiations they feel that appeals to public opinion are just a bluff. If American public opinion is contrary to what they want to do, our government or some hidden body, a "capitalist Politburo," must be manipulating it. We think of compromise as a natural way to get on with the job, but to them "compromise" is usually coupled with the adjective "rotten." They are puzzled by our emphasis on the desirability of compromise. They think we can be pushed around when we propose compromises prematurely, i.e., before they have fully tested the firmness of our positon. When we or the British advance a series of compromises, we confuse them by changing our position so often.

The Anglo-American idea of political compromise is based on the expectation of there being at least two sides to a question, so that a workable compromise represents a position somewhere between or among a series of positions each of which is sincerely believed in and stoutly defended. But the Bolshevik idea of the Line is more accurately represented by the figure of a lens which is correctly focused; there is only one correct focus for any given situation, and this is not seen as arrived at by finding some mid-point between lens readings which are too open and those which are too closed; rather, all settings except the correct focus are seen as deviations from the single correct position.

The absolute Truth embodied in the policy of the leaders had to be reconciled with the need for change. An autocratically organized society may meet the changes resulting from technological change, relative military strength in respect to other national states, etc., by simply handing down fiats from the dominating group for or against large families, universal conscription, or any other practice that it is considered necessary to initiate or alter. Such autocratic leaders may invoke, on behalf of their demands, patriotism, religion, loyalty, or fear of reprisal. Tsarist Russia and Japan previous to World War II were traditional societies of this type, and Nazi Germany was a hastily assembled twentieth-century model.

The Bolsheviks have drawn on historical autocratic models and, in phraseology, partly on Western democracy. But it has become clear that Western democratic practices, with their emphasis on the direction of government being derived from preferences which the majority of the people express among alternative courses of action, are hard to combine with the idea of a single Truth or with the overriding importance of a single power center. In the United States and Great Britain there is usually no dominant feeling for some single course's being the inevitable line of action. In Anglo-American democracy it is recognized that each next step must be felt out: "Only one link in the chain of destiny," said Churchill, "can be handled at a time."[6]

But according to Lenin, as quoted by Stalin,[7] "it is not enough to be a revolutionary and an adherent of socialism or communism in general. What is needed is the ability to find at any moment that particular link in the chain which must be grasped with all one's might to gain control of the whole chain and pass without a hitch to the next link."

The political forms of the Soviet Union today are related to this Bolshevik belief that those in power should and do have a correct diagnosis of the total historical situation and must use this power to the utmost. Authority is thus, in Bolshevik dogma, held to be justified by Truth and is to be exercised by those most able to perceive and to be most vigilant in combating, in themselves and in others, tendencies to deviate from Truth, either to the right or to the left. As the Soviet Union developed, the group of leaders allowed to express, first publicly and then behind closed doors, conflicting views as to what the correct position was, was steadily narrowed down. But the theory and its expression in purges, in political discussions, or, for example, in literary criticism seems not to have changed. At any given moment in history there is only one course of action which is right; the Party, through its leaders, perceives this right course; all must acknowledge the leaders' monopoly of the Truth at all times and the rightness of the Line at any given time, whether it concerns the tempo and method of collectivization, making a pact with a former enemy power, or shifting a metallurgical policy. The implementation in action of each change in the Line commits large numbers of people to a policy which has the authority not only of power but also of Truth. Such a policy may be evaded or revised in practice, but its over-all formulations cannot be questioned by its implementers. The ordinary channels of communication through which, in the West, the lower ranks of any complicated organization—the army, a large industry, a foreign service—question the wisdom or the practicability of a policy are closed. The Western expedient of new elections which can brand the policy of the group in power as wasteful, blind, leading straight to depression, inflation, or war is also not present. Individuals in important positions below the

---

[6] Excerpt from a speech on the Crimean Conference delivered by Winston Churchill to the House of Commons, February 27, 1945.

[7] J. Stalin, "Foundations of Leninism" (*Osnovi Leninizma*), as in Stalin, *Leninism,* New York, 1928, p. 156.

top level who execute a given policy seek to build up subsidiary power centers, insisting on the exact following of the Line, for the execution of which their present powers are held to be granted. But the very zeal which it is appropriate to show in following out the Line decreases the possibility of such lower administrators making corrections which would prevent a course of action going too far in one direction, and tends instead to push it even further along the path inaugurated at the original shift. Sooner or later, because conditions change so rapidly in an economy devoted to change, and within the present structure of world politics, it becomes necessary to shift the Line. This, according to Bolshevik theory, can be done very easily by the leaders, whose every position is justified by their ability to recognize the time at which the Line should change. However, the problems involved in a thousand subsidiary parts of the huge bureaucratic structure are not so easily disposed of. The adjustments required in different fields may take months or even a year or so to carry out, and the discrepancies in timing between different areas may themselves become a source of confusion.

Many subordinate officials who came into power at the last shift in the Line began their terms of power or office by loudly disagreeing with those whom they replaced, strongly emphasizing their allegiance to the new Line. The jobs under them were filled by those who would rigidly carry out their orders. In every field of administration, whether it be the school system or the industrial system, the editing of magazines or agricultural research, there is an accepted doctrine. These doctrines are superseded by the new Line.[8] Under the formula of displacing those who have been either too slow or too fast in adjusting to the new Line, a political house cleaning can take place. If there has been an argument within a section of the apparatus as to the exact direction to be given, for example, to work in literature, biology, or social science, and a major or even a minor shift in the Line occurs, the losing side goes out. In other words, changes in Line are usually reflected in most aspects of Soviet life, even in those which appear to have no connection with the point at issue, while shifts in the Line will be reflected in changes of personnel all down the lines of command which regulate every aspect of Soviet life. It is often hard for an outsider to see why a change in evaluation of a theory of Shakespeare's poetic method should have any link with, for example, a theory of selecting young people to be directed into factory work; and such a link may be, and is usually, expressed in denunciatory terms, by such general words as "objecti-

---

[8] For examples, see P. Mosely, "Freedom of Artistic Expression and Scientific Inquiry in Russia," *Annals of the American Academy of Political and Social Science,* Vol. 200, November, 1938, pp. 254–74; Ivan D. London, "A Historical Survey of Psychology in the Soviet Union," *Psychological Bulletin,* Vol. 46, No. 4, July, 1949, pp. 241–77; and "Theory of Emotions in Soviet Dialectic Psychology," *Feelings and Emotions,* edited by Martin L. Reymert, McGraw-Hill Book Company, Inc., New York, 1950.

vism," "formalism," "kowtowing before the bourgeois West," "equalization," "campaign style of work," etc. Meanwhile the personnel shift will express some change in the relative positions of the advocates of opposing theories, and the side which wins will work out the relationship to the Line. As many of these ideological links are very thin, it is not surprising that something which is forbidden, or out of date, or declared to be no longer correct is often more clearly stated than that which is positively approved. Even where a directive is clear, it is likely to be negatively stated. Thus a directive to document Russian precedence in intellectual history may be conveyed by a general directive against "kowtowing before the West."

Examples of the way in which changes in Line are interpreted in particular fields may be found in the professional literature of the field in question. So, in the *Teachers' Gazette*,[9] the article, "Against the Overburdening of School Children," states:

> One must accustom students to guard their own and other people's time, to give up excessive link gatherings, publishings of meaningless newspapers, albums, etc. . . . Often komsomol regional committees evaluate the activity of squads and troops not according to real educational results but according to purely superficial showing: is an exhibition handsomely presented, are wall-newspapers artistically put out, how many albums and placards are made by the pioneers. . . . It is time to protest against *formalism* in educational work. [italics ours]

Here the damning word "formalism," always an epithet of disapproval, is used to describe and condemn a particular set of educational practices. The same condemnation occurs in an article on "The Pioneers," in *Family and School*,[10] which describes the way in which a disapproved type of leader is represented as thinking:

> "Why entrust this to a new link or squad which may fulfill the task one has no idea how? It is better to give it to the one which has repeatedly proved itself in other matters," some leaders figure. "Why should I let the pioneers repair, decorate or make installations in the pioneer room when a professional worker can do it better?" so sometimes thinks a director of a school. It is such people who adjust pioneer gatherings exclusively to dates of the Revolutionary and school calendar. The needs and interests of the pioneers do not interest them. The Central Committee of VLKSM demands a decisive end of *bureaucratism* and *formalism* in pioneer work. [italics ours]

Even the way children's games are taught in school will be scrutinized and attacked:[11]

---

[9] "Against the Overburdening of School Children" (report on the meeting of the Collegium of the Ministry of Education), *Teachers' Gazette* (*Uchitel' skaya Gazeta*), November 11, 1948.

[10] V. Khanchin, "The Pioneers," *Family and School* (*Sem'ya i Shkola*), September, 1947.

[11] A. P. Usova, "On Ideology in Educational Work of Kindergartens," *Pre-School Education* (*Doshkol'noe Vospitanie*), May, 1948.

Probably janitors in all countries need the same "instruments of production," but one cannot create an image of a Soviet janitor, postman, mechanic, talking only of his implements. One must show his attitude to his work. But no games show this. Such "neutrality" of games, limitation of their subject-matter, may be justly considered as *ideological lack* (*bezideinost'*) and *political lack* (*apolotichnost'*). [italics ours]

The Party leadership is held, in Bolshevik political dogma, to owe its right to rule and its relation to Truth to its ability to foresee the future, to "hear the grass growing under the ground." The rightness of the Line is a sanction for the exercise of power, and the successful maintenance of power is a sign that the Line was true. This has meant in practice that the success of any policy assumed enormous importance in passing judgment upon it. So an informant's report of a conversation between a member of the CPSU and a German communist in 1926 was as follows:

I said to him: "How was I to know about Germany, about its economic conditions, about the ramifications of the socialist party?" (That is, that the Soviet leadership's plans for the revolution in Germany were made in ignorance of the real situation.) "I was only a young Communist. But you, you should have known." And he, twenty years older than I, said: "I did know, but who was I to tell them? They made a revolution. They made our dreams come true."

The overwhelming effect of Soviet success in stifling such criticism among non-Soviet communists in the late twenties and thirties was paralleled within the Soviet Union by the effect on the Oppositionists of Stalin's predictions coming true instead of their own. The Oppositionists had believed that catastrophe from within and from without would follow from the Line taken by the Party leadership. When this did not happen, the Oppositionists were forced to reconsider their entire position. Radek gives an account of this:[12]

"In 1934, we considered that defeat was inevitable. We proceeded from an overestimation of the difficulties in the countryside. In industry we considered that there was a transitional period when even the newly-built factories were only just being put into operation. The position on the railways was at that time considered to be catastrophic, but now, towards the end of 1935, could we consider that the situation on the railways was catastrophic? . . . I . . . knew of the opinion held of our railways by foreign intelligence services who considered that our railways were prepared for war. Could I, towards the end of 1935 . . . consider that our industry was doomed in the event of war? . . . I . . . knew that everything required for the prosecution of war would be supplied. In the case of agriculture, I myself did not have a wide field of observation: every year I went to the same collective farms, in the Kursk Guberniya . . . in 1935 [they] represented . . . something absolutely different from what

---

[12] *Report of Court Proceedings in the Case of the Anti-Trotskyite Centre* heard before the Military Collegium of the Supreme Court of the USSR, Moscow, January 23–30, 1937. Published by the People's Commissariat of Justice of the USSR, Moscow, 1937, pp. 123–24.

they were in 1933. . . . And so, if in 1933 or 1934 we proceeded from the assumption that defeat was inevitable . . . we now saw that the idea of the destruction of the USSR by western fascism and by the military-fascist circles in the east, which Trotsky took as his starting point, was now, from the standpoint of objective reality, a fantasy, that all the conditions for victory existed."

And Bukharin stated at the Third Trial:[13]

. . . everyone of us sitting here in the dock suffered from a peculiar duality of mind, an incomplete faith in his counter-revolutionary cause. I will not say that the consciousness of this was absent, but it was incomplete. Hence, a certain semi-paralysis of the will, a retardation of reflexes. . . . Even I was sometimes carried away by the eulogies I wrote of Socialist construction. . . . There arose what in Hegel's philosophy is called a most unhappy mind. . . . The might of the proletarian state . . . disintegrated its enemies from within . . . it disorganized the will of its enemies and American intellectuals begin to entertain doubts . . . in connection with the trials taking place in the USSR, this is primarily due to the fact that these people do not understand . . . that in our country the antagonist . . . has . . . a divided . . . mind. And I think that this is the first thing to be understood. I take the liberty of dwelling on these questions because I had considerable contacts with these upper intellectuals abroad. . . .

Radek looks back on his 1930–31 belief in the catastrophic consequences of rapid and forced collectivization:[14]

. . . I dissented on the main question: on the question of continuing the fight for the Five Year Plan. . . . History's joke was that I overestimated the power of resistance, the ability, not only of the mass of kulaks, but also of the middle peasants, to pursue an independent policy. I was scared by the difficulties. . . .

The effort to discern the Line becomes endowed with all the emotion generated by the desire to remain in power, and by individual commitment to the future of the Soviet Union. (For the purposes of this argument it is not necessary to attempt to assess the degree to which Stalin and his associates are influenced by one consideration as distinct from the other, or the degree to which these considerations are felt as distinct.) The smaller the group at the top, the more monolithic the structure, the simpler a shift in the Line becomes. But the problems at lower administrative levels remain. Because of the tie-in with the Line of particular administrative and technical procedures, scientific schools of thought, etc.—subjects about which substantive differences of opinion exist—the administrator who has geared his practice most articulately to the Line becomes the most vulnerable when the Line changes. We should expect to find, therefore, two trends: a demand from the top for ever more flexible,

---

[13] N. I. Bukharin, Report of Court Proceedings in the Case of the Anti-Soviet "Bloc of Rights and Trotskyites" heard before the Military Collegium of the Supreme Court of the USSR, Moscow, March 2–13, 1938. Published by the People's Commissariat of Justice of the USSR, Moscow, 1938, pp. 776–77.

[14] Report of Court Proceedings in the Case of the Anti-Trotskyite Center, Moscow, January 23–30, 1937, pp. 85–86.

unquestioning obedience, ever more explicit establishment of links between a particular practice and the general Line, and a tendency at lower levels to avoid the ideological tying-in of special procedures or issues with the Line. In a sense, the politicizing of the whole of life leads to a sort of attempted counter-depoliticization. But this depoliticization in turn is condemned by the Bolshevik leadership as a shortsighted policy which "lags behind life." So, in a discussion of current Soviet literature on the organization and planning of industrial enterprises, S. Kamenitser delivers a characteristic rebuke for such attempt to escape the dilemma. He says:[15]

> The basic defects of the . . . books examined . . . is the attempt to depart from class examination of problems of the economics and organization of enterprises, and to hide in the technical, practical side of the question. Technicism in works on production organization is not a chance phenomenon. This tendency to emasculate the class content of the work organization of the enterprise (is a tendency) to gloss over . . . the superiority of socialist enterprise.

The way the Truth, which is to be applied in every area of life, is derived, when expressed in the Line, has changed through the years. In the first years of the Soviet Power it was assumed that the Truth was arrived at through collective deliberation of the Party rather than through the deliberation of any one organ or person within it. In those years and, with diminishing effectiveness, back to 1929, "Party democracy" was supposed to mean that all members of the Party, acting through cells and then through regional and finally through All-Union Party meetings, would help the leaders "at the center" to formulate the "correct Line." Accordingly, each Party member was supposed to exercise full freedom of discussion (within the general program of the Party) until a decision had been reached by a Party Congress, and only after that was he expected to abandon all differences of opinion and work with all his strength to carry out the decision reached by the Party.

As early as the 10th Congress of March, 1921, Lenin expressed strong doubts as to whether the Party could any longer afford the great amount of effort expended in reaching decisions in this way. During the twenties, the reinforcement of control from above over Party personnel went on rapidly, and, by 1928, decisions were already reached by this means before a Party Congress was called to approve them. Thus, in official histories of the Party today, the period of the twenties, in which there were still many factions each giving an interpretation of the Truth, is passed over very rapidly, and the whole emphasis is placed on the importance of applying known Truth.

The appropriate behavior of the Party member today is to know the principles of Marxism-Leninism and to apply them as directed by the Line, not to think about them. But application must occur in every field.

---

[15] From *Planovoye Khoziaistvo*, No. 3, 1949. Quoted in *Current Digest of the Soviet Press*, No. 33, p. 25.

Stalin, as the perfect exemplar of such detailed and pervasive application, is described in a statement by Kaganovich at the 17th Party Congress, 1934:[16]

> The work on the literary front was unsatisfactory. Stalin studied the problem and he did not limit himself to pious generalizations or orders to the workers on the literary front. He went to the core of the problem. He put the question differently: It is necessary, he said, to organizationally change the situation and the question was laid down of the liquidation of RAPP [Russian Association of Proletarian Writers], of the establishment of a united Union of Writers; after this organizational solution of the question, the writing forces rose, developed, and things in literature improved. The solution of the organizational problem thus secured the application of the Party line to literature.

It follows almost inevitably, so strong is the emphasis upon the correct application of known Truth, that those who are able to apply the Line, to act in accordance with a definite directive, in terms of a body of doctrine, would seem to be more likely to survive and to arrive at positions of leadership than those who have any tendency toward questioning or doubt. This is, of course, an outstanding aspect of Stalin, that he has been able to concentrate on the application of his conception of Leninism in a state of what appears to be undisturbed orthodoxy. All doubt is pictured in contemporary Bolshevik doctrine today as leading finally to complete loss of faith, and the inevitable accompaniment of loss of faith is to become the active agent of the enemies of the Soviet Union. The threat, dramatized in the trials of the mid-thirties, and expressed over and over again at every level in the official literature, is that belief and practice are inextricably joined.

Muralov tells as follows of his development in prison:[17]

> Muralov: I reasoned that if I continued to remain a Trotskyite . . . I might become the standard-bearer of counter-revolution. This frightened me terribly. . . . Was I to remain in opposition and continue to aggravate the affair. My name would serve as a banner to those who were still in the ranks of counter-revolution. This was what decided me.
> Vishinsky: There were no prospects in the struggle?
> Muralov: The danger of remaining in these positions, the danger to the state, to the Party, to the revolution.

And Grinko says in his last plea:[18]

> I refer to my inner feeling of satisfaction . . . my happiness at the fact that our . . . conspiracy has been discovered and that the . . . calamities which we were preparing and partially carried out against the USSR, have been averted.

---

[16] L. Kaganovich, 17th Congress of All-Union CPSU (*XVII s'ezd Vsesoyuznoi Kommunisticheskoi Partii*), stenographic account, Moscow, 1934, p. 565.

[17] Report of Court Proceedings in the Case of the Anti-Trotskyite Centre, Moscow, January 23–30, 1937, pp. 232–33.

[18] Report of Court Proceedings in the Case of the Anti-Soviet "Bloc of Rights and Trotskyites," Moscow, March 2–13, 1938, p. 721.

Radek concludes his remarks at the second trial with remarks addressed to "those elements who were connected with us."[19]

> . . . the Trotskyite organization became a center for all counter-revolutionary forces; the right organization . . . is just another center for all the counter-revolutionary forces in the country.

In Bolshevik theory one cannot be a passive doubter and merely go away quietly into political oblivion and simply sit, having lost one's faith. It is considered that an individual who was once trained as a member of the Party will have so learned to combine belief and action that, if he changes his mind, he is potentially more dangerous than one who never underwent Bolshevik training. (There is always a danger also that, in the West, security agencies may act in response to this Bolshevik view and insist that individuals who leave the Party perform extraordinary services against the Party before they can become rehabilitated as repentant members of a democratic state. Such a response to this Bolshevik view tends, on the one hand, to strengthen the absolutism of Communist Party membership and, on the other, to strengthen the Soviet belief that it is unsafe to leave backsliders alive.)

This belief provides the rationale of the relentlessness with which the Soviet Union persecutes any Party member who appears to have faltered, deviated, or doubted in the slightest degree. This is not to be compared with the attitude of the Spanish Inquisition, which tortured the erring soul for that individual erring soul's sake to save it from Hell, for the individual is not regarded as valuable within the Soviet system. It is rather to be compared with the calculation of the Holy Office that, since all men "partake of one another," each erring soul would inevitably produce other erring souls and would thus contaminate the entire body of the faithful. So, by Bolshevik doctrine, the backslider cannot be let alone, because such a one will not merely backslide into harmless activity but will become transformed almost instantaneously into an active enemy. The insistence, in the Moscow trials, on the active and dangerous role of former Opposition leaders, who had actually been leading lives of political retirement and meaninglessness for several years, served to dramatize the belief that there is no neutral position for those who have once committed themselves to the Party.

The few records we have suggest that the only course of action which seemed open to Soviet foreign service officers who wished to break with the Soviet Union was to get in touch immediately with some anti-Communist or anti-Soviet group. Each dissenter who does this dramatizes in practice the Soviet leadership's belief that those who are not wholly with them are actively and totally against them. The belief that all who differ must implement their enmity leads to practices in the Party which in turn force all deviators to more extreme steps

---

[19] Report of Court Proceedings in the Case of the Anti-Trotskyite Centre, Moscow, January 23–30, 1937, p. 550.

than they would otherwise have taken. Total commitment to the Party includes the acceptance of the Party's right to sentence to death—not only as any soldier is prepared to face certain death when his commanding officer so orders, but to the point of accepting the rightness and probability of being court-martialed in disgrace and shot, although every effort was made to obey every order. This attitude can be documented most vividly from the behavior of the old Bolsheviks, such as Krivitsky. Krivitsky claims that he did not break with Moscow,[20] even when he was ordered home during the height of the Purges and knew that he would be purged. He planned to return, although he was certain that he would be liquidated. However, after he had actually boarded the train for Moscow he received a remand which made him feel that the Party had been testing him, that his willingness to return and be shot had been doubted. Then he broke. Our best material on this requirement of absolute acceptance of the Party's right to dispose of the individual comes from Old Bolsheviks. Recent interviews with Soviet DP's suggest that Party membership today often does not carry such completeness of dedication.

The emphasis appears to have shifted from the absolute devotion spontaneously accorded by the Party member to the absolute devotion demanded by the Party leadership. This demand for devotion in turn appears to be accompanied by an extreme fear that it will not be met, that the Party membership will yield to temptation.

Unless this conviction of the almost immediate and inevitable transformation of a doubting adherent into an active enemy is kept firmly in mind, the disciplining of Party members, the "reconditioning" of those returned from Western countries after the War, and the distrust of every Soviet citizen who lived under the occupation[21] are likely to be interpreted as signs of greater fear and instability in the regime than actually exist.

Americans are likely to equate the Soviet fear of the slightest expressed preference for anything Western, even the most innocent remark about some superior gadget, such as an electric switch,[22] as showing the same degree of hysteria which would have to be postulated if American officialdom became as worried by slight statements that child care or public health regulations were good in the Soviet Union. But the basic United States political position is that those who are not actively *disloyal* can be counted on to be either loyal or neutral. The Soviet denial of the possible existence of such neutral ground makes all these apparently hysterical reactions to the smallest doubt or the slightest criticism take on a very different coloring than would be the case

[20] W. G. Krivitsky, *In Stalin's Secret Service,* Harper & Brothers, New York, 1939, p. 260.

[21] Louis Fischer, *Thirteen who Fled* (subeditor, Boris A. Yakovlev; translators, Gloria and Victor Fischer), Harper & Brothers, New York, 1949.

[22] P. Antokol'sky, "About Poetry, Education of the Youth and Culture" (*O poesi, vospitanii molodykh, o kul'ture*), *Znamya,* January, 1947, p. 141.

if they occurred in the United States. It is not that such suppression of criticism does not express fear but that the degree of the fear cannot be measured by the minuteness of the deviations which arouse the whole paraphernalia of political suppression. In the United States, on the other hand, the size of the slip for which individual citizens or government officials are placed under suspicion at a given period may well be regarded as an indication of the political climate and of the amount of fear present at some echelon, possibly not the highest or the most central echelon.

It is important to distinguish between power conflicts among different sets of administrators, on the one hand, and on the other hand, between conflicts arising from originally nonpolitical issues as, for example, between the advocates of one laboratory method or another, or between two manufacturing processes, or between cotton monoculture and diversified agriculture. The political victors, after a shift in Line, are able to back up their side of the controversy, while the political losers will see their technical views go into the discard, at least temporarily. In the United States the same sort of thing occurs, within the services, when advocacy of a particular technical policy becomes associated with a contest between two different groups. When a new top appointment determines which group has won, either because the technical policies advocated by that group have been accepted or because the group itself has greater political acceptability, the policy of the other group will go temporarily into the discard, and the men who advocated it are likely to be frozen at a lower level than their service records promised. What is accomplished in the United States by the advancement of one group in preference to another is done in the Soviet Union by the liquidation (sometimes execution, sometimes only dismissal and banishment) or demotion of the group which was formerly in the saddle. Since 1938–39 there has been less physical liquidation and more temporary banishment or demotion.

This, in outline, is the relationship between the structure of political power and the political dogmas of Bolshevism expressed in the Line, which is an invention for reconciling the absolute rightness of the leaders at any given time with the need for change, and the repercussions at lower administrative levels, where the struggle for power often includes actual differences on technical matters.

BOLSHEVIK ASSUMPTIONS ABOUT HUMAN BEHAVIOR AS ABSTRACTED FROM THEORY AND PRACTICE

The following discussion is based on the hypothesis that the group of political leaders who founded and shaped the Russian Revolution represented, in ideal if not in actual character, a particular variant of the traditional Great Russian character. This Bolshevik ideal draws upon both Russian culture and that of Western Europe, but it had to be put into practice by a Party leadership which shared in various degrees, with the people whose behavior was to be altered, the traditional character. In the first two decades of the Revolution we thus have the spectacle of a group of adults who themselves varied in different ways from the traditional character—some of them having been deviants from childhood, others assuming the new ideal late in life—deliberately enforcing upon themselves a style of new behavior, at the same time trying to establish this behavior in the next generation.

In the course of this development, certain new behaviors, such as self-enforcement of ideal behavior combined with continual scrutiny by members of the group—methods appropriate to a transitional stage in the development of a new character type—became institutionalized as correct behavior. Self-criticism and mutual criticism, originally devices for maintaining behavior which had no history in the life experience of the individual, became established as conscience-quickening procedures. Also, many of the traditional orientations were displayed in new and disguised forms in the emerging behavior patterns of the Bolshevik. Among the people of the Soviet Union today we find (1) pre-Soviet traditional behavior, (2) Bolshevik behavior taken on in adulthood, and (3) new Soviet behavior grounded in childhood exposure to behaviors (1) and (2). Without intensive studies of individuals it is impossible to give complete descriptions of the way in which these three character orientations are combined in any one individual, or class, or group.

We can give an internally consistent, although limited, account of the traditional Russian character structure, which developed individuals prone to extreme swings in mood from exhilaration to depression, hating confinement and authority, and yet feeling that strong external authority was necessary to keep their own violent impulses in check. In this traditional character, thought and action were so interchangeable that there was a tendency for all effort to dissipate itself in talk or in symbolic behavior. While there was a strong emphasis on the need for certain kinds of control—by government, by parents and teachers—this control was seen as imposed from without; lacking it, the individual would revert to an original impulsive and uncontrolled state. Those forms of behavior which involve self-control rather than endurance, measurement rather than unstinted giving or taking, or calculation rather than immediate response to a situation were extremely undeveloped. The distinctions between the individual and the group and between the self and others were also less emphasized than in the West, while the organization of the *mir,* the large, extended families, and religious and social rituals stressed confession and complete revelation of self to others and the merging of the individual in the group.

With little capacity to plan, work for, and execute a long series of steps toward a goal, the traditional Russian showed a large capacity to endure adverse conditions and to respond with great completeness to the particular conditions of the moment.

Traditional Russian character assumed the coexistence of both good and evil in all individuals, and, in attitudes toward individuals, an expectation that friends could behave like enemies was combined with an expectation that this behavior could also be reversed—by confession, repentance, and restoration of the former state.

With little interest in man's particular responsibility for particular acts, the traditional Russian emphasized instead a general diffuse sense of sinfulness in which all men shared. Little distinction was made between thought and deed, between the desire to murder and the murder itself. All men were held to be guilty, in some degree, of all human crimes. Against this lack of distinction between thought and deed there was a strong emphasis upon distinctions among persons, on a purely social basis, an intolerance of any ambiguity as between superiors and subordinates. This rigidity in matters of deference and precedence, however, was relieved by a strong countertendency to establish complete equality among all human souls and to wipe out all social distinctions.

Against this description of traditional Russian character, it is possible to place a description of Bolshevik ideals, in which description it is necessary to rely a great deal more upon written statements of purpose or upon the analysis of political acts and, where there are fewer data upon the actual character of the Bolshevik leadership. In assessing the regularities in the character of the traditional Russian, it is possible to use materials pertaining to a relatively slowly changing situation, where some data on the behavior of parents and grandparents can be used to understand the behavior of children. The Bolshevik leadership group, on the other hand, were assembled from diverse backgrounds and welded hastily and painfully together; and they must be considered in terms of a set of ideals on which the effect of such personalities as Lenin and Stalin and the importance of an imported ideology, that of Hegel and Marx, both have to be taken into account. It is possible to show very striking continuities between old Russian and Soviet political behavior, as in the demand for written confessions, the demand for the confession of sins which were not committed, the relationships between leader and people, the forms of political expansionism, etc. But even here it is impossible to assay how much a new leadership, of a different character, is taking models from an old historical situation—as a man who had sat cross-legged all his life might adopt the sitting behavior appropriate for chairs when he found himself living in a house—and how much these continuities are given their form by a persistence of certain aspects of traditional Russian character in the present Bolshevik leadership.

With our knowledge of the traditional Russian character and a systematic use of the theories of dynamic psychology and cultural analysis, it is possible to relate the utterances and public behavior of the Bolsheviks to their expressed goals on the one hand and the probable persistence of traditional Russian character on the other so as to construct hypotheses about contemporary Soviet behavior.

The Bolshevik ideal personality can usefully be seen as an attempt to *counteract* tendencies in the traditional Russian character which were seen as preventing the establishment of Bolshevism and as an attempt to *introduce,* or at least to accentuate, tendencies which were recognized and admired in Western civilization. In this ideal, the individual must be goal-oriented; all acts must be seen as instrumental in reaching the final goal—the triumph of Communism —and no act must be valued only in and for itself or be judged without reference to a goal. Instead of lack of internal control, surrender to impulse, and dependence on external authority, the Bolshevik is expected to develop a strong internal conscience, an ability to produce the highest level of activity without external prodding or stimulation. By constantly pressing against the limits, by "swimming against the stream," he can establish and maintain the necessary organization of his own personality. There must be no diffuseness in his behavior, it must be continually focused and purposeful, measured, calculated, planned, and appropriate. Within his behavior there must be a rigid subordination of personal and private feeling to the demands of the final goals of the Party. Whereas the traditional Russian culture valued rest and relaxation, the Bolshevik ideal distrusts both. Rest must be transformed into a means for more effective work or be suspect.

So far, this statement of the Bolshevik ideal will be recognized as a rather generalized ideal, one which, with a very few changes, could be ascribed to the Puritan fathers of early New England or to many Protestant groups in Western Europe at periods of high self-conscious religious ferment.[23]

We may now come, however, to the more specifically Russian aspects of the Bolshevik ideal, which can in turn be related systematically to Russian history, and to theories of dynamic psychology. Ideologically, Russian Bolshevism demands a complete subjection of the individual, by an act of individual will, to the control of the Party. The individual is to have a strong, internal conscience, yet the perception of the correct line of action is delegated to a small group of leaders, and the will of the individual is to be used first for the voluntary act of initial subjection and then to execute this Truth perceived by the leadership. In organizational terms, the ties between the leader and the led reflect the older relationships between people, bureaucracy, and Tsar. In ideal political behavior, the rigid self-criticism and mutual criticism necessary to maintain a new and difficult way of life has become a regular pattern, enjoined even on those among whom, if the Soviet educational system had

---

[23] This view of the Bolshevik revolution, as embodying a kind of delayed Protestantism, together with the particular psychodynamics which accompany such changes, was developed by Erik H. Erikson. See E. H. Erikson, *Childhood and Society,* Chap. 10, "The Legend of Maxim Gorky's Youth," W. W. Norton & Company, New York, 1950.

succeeded, such efforts to overcome the old character type should have been unnecessary. In administrative behavior, the feeling that the whole structure is newly erected upon and only partially related to the earlier base is found in the fear of the leadership that any slip, any deviation, however small, will bring the whole shaky edifice crashing to the ground. Although the new character structure calls for an individual who is extremely clear about his own responsibilities and duties, Soviet administration of justice still shows a lack of interest in the actual connections between a particular criminal and a particular crime, operating instead on a theory that all are to some degree guilty—in thought if not in deed—of something. In regular administrative practice, a great deal of the cumbersomeness and inefficiency of the Soviet system is due to a failure to make individuals accountable only for that for which they are given real responsibility. Instead, an accounting is demanded from officials, agencies, or party organs of the success of a harvest or of the fulfillment of a manufacturing plan over which those held accountable had no real authority.

When we come to the third group—those who have been educated in explicit accordance with Bolshevik ideas, but by individuals, parents, teachers, older brothers and sisters who shared to a greater or lesser degree an acceptance of the new ideal character—we again have to erect our hypotheses on a structure many aspects of which are unknown. We have, however, considerable systematic knowledge of the functioning of the educational process in other cultures.

We have a description of traditional Russian character. We have an account of Bolshevik ideals. We have formal accounts of Soviet pedagogical practice, youth organizations, expected family relationships, and we have a certain amount of data, from records of DP's, on actual educational situations. Any statement regarding the character of Soviet youth, educated wholly under the Soviet regime, has to be qualified by our lack of knowledge of proportional relationships between the new ideal and the actuality. For example, present-day Soviet pedagogy stresses the importance of the biological family of father, mother, and several children, of firm parental discipline, and of responsible cooperation in the home on the part of the children, who are to be reared with a strong emphasis on strict hygienic training. It is possible to say what effects such a family structure will have—when it exists. It is also possible to outline the differences which may be expected to result in the character of children whose parents, reared in a different way, apply new educational precepts, as compared with the character resulting from the application of the same precepts by parents who have had earlier experience of, and have given complete allegiance to, the new regime. We do not, however, have enough information to know in what proportion of homes the conditions approved and propagandized by the regime actually obtain. Crowded housing, inadequate provision for the care of children of working mothers, and persistence of older attitudes toward children may to a great degree nullify the attempts of the regime to change, by education and propaganda, the character of the rising generation.

This, in brief, is an outline of the theoretical structure on which the following discussion is based. These are the three points of reference: (1) the traditional Russian character, as expressed in historical records and as analyzed by psychological methods; (2) the Bolshevik ideal character, as expressed in writing and political behavior; and (3) the emerging Soviet generation, as it can be hypothesized from our knowledge of (1) and (2), above, of Soviet formal patterns of education, of inexplicit materials from literature, and of interviews. On the basis of this general framework, particular points in Soviet attitudes toward authority have been selected for illustration and elaboration in terms of their political relevance.

On the context of these three points of reference, we have to consider the tasks confronting such a self-conscious governing group, which is attempting to maintain a society of the size and heterogeneity of the Soviet Union and at the same time to make over the character of the people. Here again the Bolshevik leadership was presented with a double problem, one outside the Party and one inside. It had to deal with the great mass of the peasants (including the small number of urban workers seldom a generation removed from peasantry), who had centuries-old habits of work and of response to authority. Inside the Party there was the problem of making over the intelligentsia, who were only to some extent westernized and who, during the last century, had built up their own peculiar forms of behavior, many of which were very antithetical to emerging Bolshevik ideals.

Among the intelligentsia, from whom the Party leadership was drawn, two trends in attitude toward the peasants can be distinguished: one toward idealization of their potentialities and the other toward an impatience with their backwardness. This latter attitude of impatient hostility toward the peasants, as being obstacles to the reconstruction of the society, was expressed in endorsements of the harshness of the forced collectivization.

In the case of the peasants, the problem was one of transforming people, who had very little interest in time, a great capacity for endurance, no experience with machines, very special habits of working in groups, a limited time perspective and a limited mobility, into competent workers in a society which was to be rapidly industrialized, workers who would have an allegiance to and mobility within the nation. The conspicuous problem with regard to the intelligentsia was one of shifting the emphasis from speculative talk to controlled action, from an interest in a vague eternal Truth, ever to be sought and never found, to a concentrated, unflagging, effortful attention to one urgent and immediate task after another. There was, of course, a relationship between the peasant who, as factory worker, had to be threatened with six months' imprisonment for coming late to work in order to impress him at all with the importance of punctuality, and the intellectual who was more interested in long discussions of Bolshevik theory than in the question of organizing propaganda for increased production in a certain industry at a certain moment. The Bolshevik demand made on both was for a new focus, a new definiteness, a new stiffening and particularizing of purpose and behavior.

An important element in contemporary Soviet practices designed to make Soviet citizens into new types of men and women is the assumption that each individual carries within him a whole series of disallowed attitudes. Self-criticism, an essential Bolshevik practice designed for continuous scrutiny of motives and behavior, covers two activities: the criticism of the self and the criticism of any member of a group by other members of the group. In both cases alertness against the appearance of evil is enjoined. Each individual (outside of the condemned "classes") is seen as having capacities for great goodness—currently, the capacity to submit all of himself voluntarily to that perfectly wise, foresighted authority, Stalin and the Party, and to exercise a maximum of initiative in the context set by the Party—but, equally, each is seen as having the capacity to become an "enemy of the people."

This belief in the possibility of the Soviet citizen's having within him the capacity to be a complete enemy is vividly dramatized in the Soviet film *Frontier*. The hero, a tiger hunter on the Manchurian border, kills four kinds of enemies in the course of the picture: six Russian traitors who have helped two Japanese to smuggle dynamite over the frontier to blow up a new industrial development, the two Japanese who have brought the dynamite and plotted an uprising, a maniac leader of a sect which has opposed Collectivization, *and* his best friend, a tiger hunter like himself, who has been his closest comrade for forty years and who in the end turns out to have betrayed the Soviet Union. In this film, the enemy without and the enemy within are identified together. The hero and the traitor he executes look almost exactly alike, have been companions all their lives, and have the *same* life history. This same theme is expanded in the postwar Soviet film *The Young Guard*, in which the whole group of young partisans are destroyed because they trusted one of their number who had been a schoolmate and whose family were all Communists.

Instead of a conception of character in which, through a long period of maturation, the individual becomes permanently attached to the Good as his society sees it and so becomes permanently incorruptible and reliable, the conception is that every individual maintains the capacity for complete betrayal of all those values to which he has hitherto shown devoted allegiance. The "enemy of the people" is the replica, in every detail, of the most devoted Soviet citizen or Party member. This gives the whole problem of authority a very special character in the need for continuous watchfulness over adults as well as children, over the high Party official as well as the humblest non-Party member, in a never-ending effort to hold the personality attached to the Good—to the Party—and to prevent the treacherous, destructive elements which are *always there,* in all personalities, from obtaining any degree of, and hence complete, control. There is no real distinction made between the watch which one should keep upon oneself, the vigilance with which the slightest doubt should be identified and extirpated in one's own mind, and the watch which should be kept upon others. This gives the peculiar collaborative tone to Soviet domestic espionage, the expectation that he who is denounced and he who denounces him are joined together. In the film mentioned above, *Frontier*, it is the victim, the enemy of the people, who is to be executed by his best friend and near double, who chooses the spot where his best friend is to execute him.

The interweaving of the ideas of watchfulness over the self and watchfulness over others is well illustrated in an interview with an informant who had been a Party member living in special quarters in Moscow, who described the method by which a member of each cell was appointed to spy on all the other cell members:

> *Question:* Did you try to find out who *was* the watcher?
>
> *Answer:* No, there was always a kind of respect for everything done by the Party. There is respect for the decision of the cell which is the decision of the Party and there is the conviction that you would do the same if they would ask you, so why should you find out? As soon as you feel insulted by the Party you are on the way out, morally.
>
> *Question:* But wouldn't it be better to know so that you don't have to worry about all the people?
>
> *Answer:* No. NO! You had better worry, engage in self-criticism, watch your-self, and if there is anybody [watching you], you don't know who it is. It is none of your business to find out. And if they tell you there is something wrong with you, you will believe it. After all you are only good so long as the Party says so. So if the Party says you are no good there must be some-thing to it.

To the Western mind, political trials in which some highly placed official is not only accused of present deviation from the Line but is also "exposed" as having always been a professional agent for a number of foreign intelligence services sound absurd. In Soviet language this is simply a way of saying that this particular accused person shall not be allowed a political comeback. Hence the indictment is phrased in such a way as to insist that there never was any good in him. The appropriate sequel to an official declaration that an individual is completely evil is his removal from society by physical liquidation.

At lower levels, purges and removals from office may be a way of stating that the individual who has so enthusiastically executed a past Line is not capable of changing to the new Line. His very commitment to the previous Line becomes the ground for alleging that he has always been an enemy, which ground is often paradoxically expressed by an accusation that his previous activity was the exact opposite of what it actually was.

The intricacies of the path by which Stalin gained control of the entire Party apparatus reflect the interrelationships between the changing Line and the possibility that any given individual may at any moment be wholly loyal or wholly an enemy. One of the steps by which Stalin gained control of the Central Committee was to keep in the Committee members of the opposition who thus became involved in unanimous decisions in favor of policies which they were denouncing in confidential discussions within high Party circles.

The way the Line is operated means that behavior which was true and loyal yesterday may be branded as false and disloyal tomorrow. The assumption that every human being is potentially and continuingly wholly good *and* wholly bad throughout life is grounded in traditional Russian character and complements political practice very neatly. All those who are unable to shift satisfactorily when the Line changes can be seen to be those in whom evil has become dominant. But this change is not irreversible. A man whose particular scientific dogma has been in disgrace for a period of years may be suddenly brought back from an ignominious sojourn on the periphery—a mild form of exile—and made the head of an important institute or bureau. He may be publicly described as being entirely good, while the man he replaces, who may have received the same appointment with a comparable statement of his absolute loyalty and goodness five years before, is now unmasked as having always been an "enemy of the people," or whatever the official terms of vilification may be for the exponent of the previously approved and now abandoned course of action.

In fields less specialized than the arts and sciences, a capable man who has been displaced from one position and demoted or banished to the periphery but not physically liquidated may reappear later in some quite different field. Since 1938–39 there appears to have been less physical liquidation and more banishment to the periphery with possibilities of return to positions of importance at a later date. This relaxation may be due partly to the extreme shortage of trained personnel, especially since World War II, partly to some relaxation in the Soviet demand that individuals be defined as wholly good or wholly bad at any given time, and partly to a partial return to the more traditional Russian acceptance of the inherent goodness and badness in each individual.

This belief, that each individual is capable simultaneously of all good and all evil, is also associated with a great deal of confusion in role. In Soviet behavior there may be seen an extreme defense against this mixture of roles, a struggle between the attempt to keep each individual's role clear and a tendency to treat each individual as capable of playing any part—from hero to traitor, from prosecutor to defendant, or from victim to executioner. The interrogators in the great trials were, to a considerable extent, persons who knew that they themselves would be liquidated very soon, and yet it was felt at the top that this knowledge would not materially detract from their efficiency as interrogators. There is a conspicuous lack of official executioners in the political police; members of the apparatus of many different levels might have to officiate as executioners. And within the Party cell, an individual might be selected to spy, but, if not so officiating, he would be spied upon.

In the film, *Frontier,* which is primarily concerned with this confusion of roles, there is not only the drama of virtual identity between the faithful Soviet citizen and the traitor, but also a ragged little peasant, who plays the role of inspirational speaker, of spy and informer, and who describes himself as "a little bit of a GPU."

There have been a variety of devices used to deal with the problems which arise from confusion of roles and the continuing possibilities of treachery. One device is to simplify the demands made upon the rank-and-file Party member, who is no longer expected to understand as much of the ideology as he was in the past. This makes the role of rank-and-file member simpler; it is easier to treat him like a sentry, taking him off one assignment and giving him different orders for a new turn of sentry duty. The narrowing of authority at the top, from Party Congresses through Central Committee to concentration in the Politburo, also serves to reduce the diffusion of possible treachery at upper levels. The narrowing of authority, however, also increases the demands made on each individual in authority and, by increasing the scope and range of his activities and responsibilities, increases the gravity of a breakthrough of disallowed behavior. So an individual, such as Yezhov, who is entrusted with great power to liquidate others must in turn be liquidated.

The contrast between the potential dangers inherent in any whole personality and the greater safety involved in rigidly prescribed and specialized functions is repeated over and over again at the organizational level. A complete range of functions is assigned to such large, unmanageable groups as Party Congresses, Plenums, District Committees, which break down into factions amid mutual accusation and suspicion. An attempt is made to correct this by setting up a narrower group which can exercise a particular function without breakdown. This organizational characteristic was used by Stalin to gain control of the Politburo: when he wished to reduce the power of the Plenum of the Central Committee, he increased its size, at the same time giving it more functions to perform and so making it less capable of performing them. Many of the functions of responsibility for political security, which were part of the regular duties of Party members in the twenties and thirties, seem now to be delegated to the political police (in the Ministries of Internal Affairs and State Security), who therefore are in the position of watching the Party. There are also special Party cells within the political police to watch them in turn and to keep them under the control of the Party. The political police force is now said to contain over 1,500,000 members and to have doubtfully adequate methods of checking on new recruits. This inadequacy is presented as being compensated for by the close watch that the political police keep on one another. The question immediately arises: "Who watches them?" Of course, this continual tendency of the specialized function of preservation of security to break down is partly associated with the very nature of any security system, but the types of confusions and reversals characteristic of Soviet assumptions regarding human behavior exacerbate it.

One of the most curious features of the Soviet system has been the combination of the willingness to condemn an individual to death, to define him as totally an enemy, in terms of some small past action, and the absence of any really functioning modern system of keeping track of suspected persons. Generalized terror, mass arrests, indiscriminate accusations take the place of careful modern police work which might actually identify a particular saboteur. The actual nexus between any given crime and any given person is exceedingly weak. For all crimes there must be identified criminals; but the accused need not have committed the particular crime, since they are, at all events, capable of any crime and have probably committed—at least in intent—other crimes. Because of the looseness of the police system, and the willingness to pin any accusation on to any convenient breast, sabotage, espionage, and temporary escape from the vigilance of particular police are comparatively easy, so that the need for more terror as a controlling measure which also makes any final escape less possible is intensified. The most recent evidence suggests that the system of police controls is being tightened although not necessarily made more specific.

The complications involved in assuming that every individual can be held accountable for anything which occurs, regardless of his specific responsibility, are shown vividly in Soviet theories of industrial organization, especially when these theories are compared with contemporary press accounts of failures and malpractice in factory organization. Soviet theories of industrial organization insist that organization is something which can be imposed upon a group of individuals, each of whom will be totally involved in the particular role he has to play, whether that of worker, foreman, or manager. This means that not only the particular parts of the personality needed for the particular task, but also all the other always present and contradictory elements in the personality are regarded as present. Then, in accordance with Bolshevik demands, organizational theory also insists that each individual must be presented with clear-cut goals and responsibilities. Clear-cut responsibilities are necessarily limited responsibilities, involving carefully defined lines of command and subordination. Thus Soviet organizational theory and practice struggle continually to devise an organizational chart which will define and limit responsibility. But within such an organizational scheme the worker is expected to respond, not with a careful delimited measured response to the particular demands of his job, but with total devotion and spontaneity. This spontaneity, which is fed by a desire to identify with the leader, holds the danger that this is in effect identification with someone who is unrestrained by the restraints which are binding on his immediate superior. In terms of such devotion he is expected to be able to criticize his superiors and to surpass them by displaying more initiative and more activism than they.

In contrast, American theory, based on a belief in the individual's capacity to adjust to an economic role and that this will involve only part of his personality, one clear role among many roles, tends to concentrate initially on the technical aspects of the activity itself. An American organizational blueprint therefore tends to be concerned with the mutual adjustments of various technical roles.

Furthermore, in Soviet theory there is very little differentiation between different kinds of organization, as they all are seen as expressions of universal principles which combine subordination to authority with the expression of spontaneity, and every group therefore presents the same problem and the same need for organizational control as every other group. Organizational absurdities which attempt to deal with this dilemma result. Kaganovich, at the 17th Party Congress, 1934, gave the following example:[24]

> A factory in Dnepropetrovsk had 75 paid workers in the Party organization which had 5 echelons and 11 sectors. Each shop cell had 11 sectors: (1) culture propaganda, (2) mass agitation, (3) cadres, (4) verification and fulfillment, (5) work with Party *activ,* (6) works with Party candidates, (7) sector for learning vanguard role of communist for production, (8) work among komsomols, (9) work among women, (10) sector of cooperation and (11) Party dues.
>
> The matter went to such an absurd level that a link cell which had 7 Party members and 5 candidates established a bureau of the cell into which all the Party members went, and for these 7 Party members, 10 sectors were established.

Thus we see that the attempt to narrow and simplify particular functions came into continual conflict with the acceptance of the total involvement of the whole personality, so that, after eleven separate tasks had been defined in order to separate them, the same people were then required to perform all eleven.

Another illustration of the confusion of roles and of the conflict between specialization of function and the attempt to make everyone responsible for everything can be found in the management of collective farms where separate organizations, (1) Raion[25] party secretary, (2) MTS,[26] (3) Raion section of the Ministry of Agriculture, (4) Raion soviets, (5) Raion party committee of propaganda and agitation, and sometimes (6) the local bank are accountable and hence are forced into attempting to take responsibility for the harvest.

This Soviet assumption that the opposite of any form of behavior is also always potentially present is significant in interpretation of Soviet behavior in international relations. Those who have dealings with Soviet officials in international negotiations or in joint occupation councils have been struck by the

---

[24] Kaganovich, *op. cit.,* p. 556.
[25] District.
[26] Machine Tractor Station.

sudden reversals of policy which affect every aspect of every relationship, every echelon from general to chauffeur. These sudden switches are often explained in terms of the great centralization of power in the Soviet Union or the small amount of leeway allowed to any individual in the system. But while the perfect synchronization of such switches in behavior from extreme uncooperativeness to the sudden semblance of cooperation may be thus explained, the disposition to engage in sharp reversals needs further study. When the behavior of members of different societies is compared, we find that the capacity for reversing a position differs very much, from the Japanese prisoner, who is willing to broadcast on behalf of his captor within a few hours after being taken prisoner, to a people like the Poles, who remain actively intransigent in spite of drastic changes in circumstances. What is there in contemporary Soviet character which makes sudden reversals of policy sufficiently congenial that they can be carried out swiftly and easily?

We have already seen how abrupt changes in the Line and the accompanying liquidation of those persons who have most zealously and rigidly carried out the former Line are congruent with the Soviet assumption regarding human nature. Reversals are part of the mechanism of shifts in Line. Throughout the theory of Leninism-Stalinism there is an allowance for sudden sharp reversals rather than for slow gradual adjustment. There is a tendency to state extreme alternatives and to view both alternatives as part of the same system. It would be reasonable in judging, from the American point of view, for example, the expected behavior of Great Britain as an ally to say: From such and such a degree of present friendliness and cooperativeness we may expect no more than a given amount of coolness to develop, given certain conditions, over a given period of time. But a different type of estimate has to be made in the case of the Soviet Union, where the possibility of an extreme reversal is always present. As opposite and seemingly completely contradictory attitudes are already present, there is no need to allow for a transition from one to another in the behavior of officials who must execute the new policy. The typical Soviet figure of speech is to unmask, in one gesture; one position, that of friend, is replaced by a diametrically opposite one, that of enemy.

Fadeyev, in *The Young Guard*,[27] published in 1945, describes the new generation as follows:

> The seemingly most incompatible traits, dreaminess and efficiency, flights of fancy and practicality, the love of good and relentlessness—mercilessness, depth wideness of the soul and judicial calculations, passionate love of earthy happiness and reserve—these seemingly incompatible traits together create the unique countenance of the new generation.

Whereas for many Westerners the existence of one attitude—trust, cooperativeness, reliance, etc.—toward a co-worker, a superior or a subordinate, makes the

---

[27] Fadeyev, "The Young Guard," in *Znamya,* February–December, 1945.

expectation of the occurrence of the opposite attitude less likely, in Soviet expectation the closer the relationship and the greater the trust, the greater the danger, the more possible a betrayal, and the greater the need for suspicion. This seems to be a specific Stalinist trend. During the Leninist era there was an attempt to treat the world as being divided into two rather distinct parts: the world outside the Party, which was to be regarded with maximal suspicion, and the world inside the Party, where such suspicion was to be held in abeyance until proof of betrayal was provided. This Stalinist trend toward suspicion of those within can be seen as expressing, in a new form, the traditional Russian assumption that all individuals are potentially both good and evil.

This whole view of human nature is so very unfamiliar to Americans that only by the greatest attention can it be held in mind. In interpreting Soviet behavior toward the outside world, there is a tendency to say that only negative feelings are real, or, conversely, that only the periodic accommodation attitudes are real. Actually neither is real in our sense of the term, that is, in the extent to which they exclude their opposites. The situation is further complicated by the fact that Soviet policymakers require of themselves the subduing of both positive and negative feelings in the service of maximizing their power and fulfilling their exalted mission in the world. All they can admit to themselves is that they are deliberately making pretenses of friendliness or hostility.

This complex of attitudes, a habitual expectation that contradictions will coexist in such a way that any feeling may at any moment be completely replaced by its opposite, combined with the Bolshevik insistence on the subordination of both types of feeling, makes for attitudes in the leadership which seem lacking in consistency, integrity, and sincerity.

As consistency and sincerity are regarded by Americans as essential to integrity, and as both are lacking in the behavior of the Soviet leadership, there is a temptation to continue to apply American standards of judgment and to regard Soviet behavior as insincere, cynical, in the American sense, and so without integrity. This interpretation is strengthened by those Russians who reject the Bolshevik ideal and themselves accuse the Soviets of insincerity and cynicism. But from the Bolshevik point of view the essential virtue consists in being so goal-oriented (*tseleustremenyi*) that no contradiction can arise between behavior demanded by changes in the Line and the individual behavior—in a diplomat or officer on a border—needed to implement the Line. When, in attempting to interpret abrupt changes in the degree of friendliness or of distrustful reserve expressed by individual Soviet officials, we invoke ideas which attempt to distinguish between *when* they are sincere or when they are insincere, or when we regard Soviet high officials as *only* ruthlessly seeking positions of power quite regardless of any ethical implications, we lose sight of the Bolshevik ethic. In this ethic, all acts commanded by the Party are ethical because of the long-term ethical goal of a good society. In such a pursuit of ethical goals, there is both a degree of self-justification and a need for continuous self-rejustification which does not exist for those who have no such goals.

In contacts between the Soviet Union and other nationals, officials at various levels are required by the exigencies of the Line to assume different and contradictory forms of behavior. The more flexible they are in doing so, the more integrity—or perhaps "integralness" would be a better word—they have as Bolsheviks. Assumptions which Americans make about the significance of the behavior of individual Soviet officials become imponderable but very important elements in shaping the course of relationships between the United States and the Soviet Union. If judgments of Soviet official behavior by American officials are related, not to the degree of sincerity or of cynicism in our terms, but, instead, to the degree to which each Soviet official is more or less a real Bolshevik, a much higher level of sophistication is introduced.

In the above discussion, we have dealt with the Bolshevik demand that Party members and high officials subordinate their beliefs to Party goals to such an extent that any prescribed belief can easily replace another, the convictions for either being based not on the personal feelings of the individual, but on the extent to which he is prepared to act in the interests of the Party. When we examine published propaganda materials directed at the general population, we find a decreasing tolerance here also for the coexistence of contradictory and potentially oscillating attitudes. Films such as *Frontier*, made in the thirties, and *The Young Guard*, made in the forties, reveal that the fear of such coexisting feelings is still present. However, the educational propaganda attempts to direct one set of attitudes, the positive ones—absolute loyalty, devotion, and love toward the State, the Party, Stalin—and to channel hatred toward the enemy. Instead of the diffuse hatred centering on generalized qualities and impersonal forces which characterized the pre-Soviet Russian, there is an attempt to fix these attitudes on specific individuals or nations. The assumption of coexistence is still found, however, in the insistence that love and hate are in fact inseparable. Yermilov[28] comments thus:

> The heroes of the play know that the feelings of hatred towards Fascism are sacred. They are the reverse of the love of mankind. One who is not able to hate is not able to love.

In an article[29] in the Leningrad monthly *Tridtsat Dnei*, the writer watched

> . . . faces, new faces. The passions of the revolutionary, the élan of the fighter, the grit of the commander, and then love, love of life, love of its classes, of people who are builders, then the hatred of the enemy, furious, irrepressible— all this lay in new fashion upon the faces. All this penetrates deeply and organically into the faces of our men, the new men—I watched the eyes—they began to *burn* but the faces are *cold*. [italics ours]

[28] V. Yermilov, "Test through Peace" (*Ispytanie mirom*), *Literaturnaya Gazeta*, December 15, 1946, p. 2.
[29] "People of the Thirties" (*Lyudi tridtsatykh godov*), *Tridtsat Dnei*, 1935.

An article in *Molodoi Bol'shevik* declares:[30]

> Soviet patriotism includes—carries in itself (*vkluchat*) the feeling of hot hatred
> towards the enemies of our native land.

The pupils in Soviet schools must

> . . . realize that the feeling of Soviet patriotism is saturated with irreconcilable
> hatred towards the enemies of Socialist society. . . . It is necessary to learn not
> only to hate the enemy, but also to struggle with him, in time to unmask him
> and finally, if he does not surrender, to destroy him.[31]

This official attempt to direct active hatred toward the enemy as a way of
keeping love for the Soviet Union clear has its repercussions in the feeling of
these same officials that people of other countries hate the Soviet Union. "Comrade Lenin himself said: 'Are we not in an ocean of hatred?' "[32]

The official insistence on the success of this effort to separate out feelings
which are believed to coexist goes to further lengths. An educator boasts:[33]

> In all epochs children play war, usually presenting cruelty and violence. But
> our children's play at the Patriotic War reflects the noble role of the Soviet
> Army and calls forth noble feelings. There is not a single game in which
> children attacked, exhibited cruelty, violence. They always free and defend the
> motherland, chase the foe. These games express hate of violence and cruelty,
> of invaders.

For some peoples, ardent patriotic love of their own country is compatible
with moderate affection for other countries, which only extreme conditions in
the midst of war can turn into hatred. Even at the height of the Blitz against
Britain there was very little expressed hatred for Germany or attempt on the
part of the government to build hatred. Hatred of the Japanese grew gradually
among American troops, accompanying battle experiences. The Soviet leadership
seems to be seeking a way of directing coexisting love and hate. Strength of love
and strength of hate are treated as functions of each other, so that, as hatred is
directed against the enemy, love of country will increase, and vice versa.

Related to this habit of including opposite types of feeling within a single
wider attitude, of always allowing for the coexistence of opposites which makes
Soviet domestic and intra-Cominform behavior so baffling to the West, is the
type of thinking which can be described briefly as "all or none thinking." We
have already discussed the belief that if anything is wrong, then everything is

---

[30] "Educating Soviet Patriotism in the Schools," *Molodoi Bol'shevik*, December, 1947.

[31] G. Counts and N. Lodge, *I Want to be like Stalin*, The John Day Company,
New York, 1947. (Translated from V. P. Yesipov and N. K. Gocharov, official Soviet
textbook on pedagogy, published with approval of Ministry of Education, RSFSR, 1946.

[32] V. Ozerov, "The Image of a Bolshevik in the Post-War Soviet Literature," *Bol'shevik*, No. 10, May, 1949.

[33] D. Menderitskaya, "Influence of the Educator on Content of Children's Play,"
Pre-School Education (*Doshkol'noe Vospitanie*), August, 1948.

wrong, or will be almost immediately. If someone is not completely a friend, then he is completely an enemy. The smallest slip will lead to total betrayal. Says *Komsomol'skaia Pravda*:[34]

> The Komsomol must in every way improve the ideological work among the young . . . ! . . . *any* belittling of socialist ideology, Lenin teaches, *any* departure from it, signifies the same thing as strengthening bourgeois ideology. [italics ours]

There are no stable intermediate positions: one little slip from total loyalty, and nothing can stop the change from friend into enemy, from loyal Party member into traitor and spy. This lack of belief in the stability of any middle position is accompanied by the impermissibility of referring to it in any way, in contempt for the Social Democrat idea of a "middle way," and in statements that "There is no third way."

The good Communist, Basargin, in Simonov's 1947 novel, says:[35] "I wonder whether you know that all our friends with reservations become in the end most often our enemies."

The inevitable final transformation of those who begin to deviate then follows. Stalin,[36] on March 3, 1937, said:

> It should be explained to our Party comrades that the Trotskyites who represent the active element in the diversionist wrecking and espionage work of a foreign Intelligence Service have already long ceased to be a political trend, in the working class . . . that they have turned into a gang of wreckers, diversionists, spies, assassins, without principles and ideals working for the foreign Intelligence Services.

And he continues: "Against such total enemies . . . not the old methods, the methods of discussion, but the new methods, methods of smashing and uprooting, must be used."

There is a very natural tendency in the West to interpret these accusations and denunciations as nothing but political rhetoric. There is abundant evidence that the particular charges made in the trials of the Old Bolsheviks, of sabotaging the railway system, of putting glass in the butter, or of espionage for foreign intelligence services, were palpably untrue. But what Stalin (or Vishinsky, in the trials) is saying is that those who are not totally for us are totally against us. The accident that they have not committed the particular extreme act which is used illustratively in accusing them is irrelevant. American misunderstanding of this type of thinking shows up sharply when American spokesmen waste their energies in getting angry at the inaccuracies of Soviet accusations and spend heat and time in denying and disproving particular points. When a Soviet

[34] *Komsomol' skaia Pravda*, March 31, 1949, p. 2.
[35] K. Simonov, "The Smoke of the Fatherland" (*Dym otechestva*), *Novyi Mir,* November, 1947.
[36] J. Stalin, *Mastering Bolshevism*, report to the 1937 Plenum of the Central Committee of the CPSU, printed in *Bol'shevik*, April 1, 1937.

speaker in the United Nations accuses the United States of particular acts of espionage, warmongering, etc., he is saying, in effect: We are at present classifying you as a total enemy who is, if serious, undoubtedly doing, or should be doing, everything in your power against us; as we, when we classify you as a total enemy, are doing everything in our power against you. If this is recognized, the accusations can be taken as a catalogue of the hostile acts which the Soviet Union is either engaged in, or wishes us to think it is engaged in, or wishes it were able to execute. Answering speeches can be directed to the issue in dispute, while specific denials of charges can be made for the benefit of those other peoples who, like ourselves, think it necessary to deny false charges from any national group with which they are not actively at war. Such denials are, of course, exceedingly important in countering Soviet anti-American propaganda outside the Soviet Union.

Soviet assumptions about transformations from the position of total goodness to total evil may also be found in Soviet treatment of allies. All rival power centers in the world are regarded by the Kremlin as basically hostile, centers which can at best be temporarily negotiated with for truces or for purposes of combined pursuit of limited goals. And within the area of Soviet domination there is always the possibility of a formerly dutiful part of the Soviet side being transformed into the total enemy, as in the case of Yugoslavia at present.

Even with a sound, practical recognition that national states are self-interested groups, moved by considerations of power, there is a widespread expectation in the West that it is possible to set up relatively lasting good relations with other nations, and that difficulties may be overcome within such a generally good understanding. This is particularly true when relations between states have reached the formal treaty state which Americans take exceedingly seriously. The spectacle of a Soviet Union which makes a fifty-year pact with one of its satellites and denounces it two or three years later seems to us so shocking, so completely unethical, that it is likely to lead to the conclusion that there is no possibility of negotiating with such an unprincipled leadership. If it is once recognized that the friendly, nominally independent power within the Soviet orbit, with which the Soviet Union at a given moment negotiates, is also—at that moment—recognized as being potentially an extremely hostile power, it can almost be said that the Soviet Union is signing a pact with the other power as a totally loyal ally and is simultaneously including the possibility that this power may—at any time—require as formal a denunciation as a total enemy. This simultaneous acceptance of loyalty and treachery is self-evident to the Soviet leaders. It remains for further research to determine to what degree the Communist-dominated parties of neighboring countries, with cultural expectations about human nature which differ from the Bolshevik assumption, find this expectation to be either natural or monstrous.

However, this expectation, of possible transformations of allies into enemies and of the most extreme and drastic transformations following from the smallest slip, the least doubt, the slightest disloyalty, is accompanied by the possibility that they may be transformed back again. This expectation was much stronger in the early days of the Party, when the emphasis upon repentance, confession, and conversion, now reserved for the lower ranks of the Party and the Komsomols, existed at top Party levels. (What appears to be—though material on this is very scant—a recent tendency for demoted persons to have some sort of a comeback seems to apply only to the lower and middle levels of officialdom.) From the middle twenties to the middle thirties, Party behavior expressed a belief in the possibility of being an Oppositionist without becoming automatically an enemy of the Party. This expressed belief shifted in the middle thirties to an expressed belief that the transformation of an Oppositionist into a wrecker, spy, and traitor was inevitable and irreversible. This belief in irreversibility, unthinkable in the twenties, made mass liquidations within the Party possible. There have been recent signs that the process could be reversed posthumously, as in the recent interchanges between the CPSU and the Communist Party of Yugoslavia, in which Trotsky is no longer described as having been totally bad from the beginning. So, in the letter of March 27, 1948, from the CPSU to the CPY, we find this passage:[37]

> Again we might mention that, when he decided to declare war on the CPSU, Trotsky also started with accusations of the CPSU as degenerate, as suffering from the limitations inherent in the narrow nationalism of great powers. Naturally he camouflaged all this with left slogans about world revolution. However, it is well known that Trotsky himself *became degenerated, and when he was exposed, crossed over* into the camp of the sworn enemies of the CPSU and the Soviet Union. [italics ours]

Here a possible reversible period in Trotsky's early disaffection is implied by way of suggesting the possibility of a reversal in Tito's catastrophic progress toward becoming a total enemy. On the other hand, Soviet publications during late 1949 also quoted frequently from Stalin's 1938 denunciatory speeches.

We have already mentioned the tendency to banish and later to recall individuals who have shown signs of deviation. This is another instance of a possible relaxation in the extreme attitude of the thirties and a return to an older Russian expectation that, as possibilities of both total good and total evil are always present, transformation may proceed in either direction and need not be permanent. This older attitude was characteristic of pre-Soviet friendship but altered markedly after the Soviet regime was initiated. The way in which individual deviations are regarded—as committing the individual to a course of unredeemable villainy or as merely one step on a road from which full return is possible—will be one of the decisive elements in the development of the Soviet system

---

[37] *Soviet-Yugoslav Dispute,* Royal Institute of International Affairs, London, 1948, p. 15.

of authority during the next decades, and every effort should be made to obtain as much material on the subject as possible.

Within this framework of attitudes, the Soviet leadership is often involved in what looks to the West like exceedingly contradictory behavior, between their acceptance of those conditions which are believed to be absolutely given by History and the Nature of Man, on the one hand, and, on the other hand, their acceptance of their responsibility to exercise complete control, both over themselves and over others. While the Line is merely an expression of correct perception of what already exists, the execution of the Line becomes something completely within the power of the Party. If the Line is correctly perceived, then the Party is acting within the course which History must take and so has, theoretically, complete power to realize the course which has been perceived as "objectively possible." This view lends itself to fantasies of omnipotence, of invincibility. But the opposite face of these fantasies is strengthened also by the fear of the perfectly perceived, absolutely controlled situation getting out of hand, if the perception should be spoiled in execution, if a single slip between cup and lip occurs. The overestimation of power over events and over persons is thus balanced at every turn by an overestimation of the forces which may also be arrayed against the Party, against the leadership, against the Soviet Union. The burden of being perfectly right must be carried like a precariously balanced container of water, from which one drop spilled will be fatal. It is in this sense that it is possible to say that the Soviet leaders are sincerely convinced that every single thing they do is right and necessary and also that there is danger in questioning any particular act: they are frightened that they or those who follow them may, by such questioning, lead the Party and the Soviet Union to total destruction.

BOLSHEVIK WILLINGNESS TO ACCEPT OR TO FABRICATE TOKEN EVENTS

In Tsarist Russia there were attempts to give an appearance of reality and solidity to matters of dubious truth, as in the great insistence on written confessions as early as the seventeenth century or in the Potemkin villages specially set up to satisfy the demands of Catherine the Great for speedy development of the newly acquired province of Novorussiya.

These earlier customs of theatrical enactment of that which was desired by those in power or by their subordinates have become very marked characteristics of the Soviet regime. In Bolshevik doctrine, what the leadership decides shall be done is what History has already ordained is going to happen (although it is also what needs the utmost effort to make it happen). Hence, any gap between what is ordered and what occurs is proportionately less bearable. Although Bolshevik doctrine also includes stern exhortations to sobriety and recognition of facts as "stubborn things," and although romantic overoptimism is one of the condemned characteristics of the Left, nevertheless a great variety of falsifications and theatrical enactments of the ardently desired or deeply feared do occur.

This acceptance of falsification shows itself in the sort of reports which are passed up through channels in a bureaucracy reporting overfulfillment of a plan, when the overfulfillment of, for example, the readiness of the machines in a Machine Tractor Station is of such a nature that half of the tractors may break down within a week. The Machine Tractor Station will, however, already have celebrated its overfulfillment and the appropriate higher levels will have been able to include its success in their reports of their successes. Although bureaucratic conditions are particularly favorable to the tendency to believe what it is most comfortable to believe, this particular type of belief goes to special lengths in the Soviet Union. As so many of the reports are concerned with real events —the amount of grain harvested, the number of trucks turned out by a factory— false reporting has very real repercussions in actuality and so can be branded as sabotage. But as failure to overfulfill a plan may also be regarded as sabotage, the possibility of such repercussion hardly discourages the practice of inaccurate reporting.

The falsification takes many forms, even within a single factory. One informant described his wife's experience: she worked in a silk artel which listed itself as a whole as overfulfilling the plan by 110 per cent, when actually the plan had been only 65 per cent fulfilled. Within this artel, his wife's unit had actually overfulfilled by 250 per cent, but this was only credited as 121 per cent, since over 120 per cent warranted a premium. Such attempts to establish groups within which the weak can lean on the strong, as when one kolkhoz borrows from another, are very frequently reported.

Periodically the falsifications produce difficult situations. An informant described a province in which one county showed a grain delivery of 131 per cent, and, as a result, Moscow ordered that more white bread should be baked and sold in the county center. The county started to obey this order, but by the middle of the year there was no grain left. The province looked over the invoices and pointed out that several thousand kilos of grain should be left. In order to straighten out the matter, the county party committee took grain away from some of the collective farms in the county.

Even with the extreme frequency with which this type of falsification occurs in the Soviet Union, it might be regarded as merely a sign of inefficiency or corruption or graft, if it were not for many other Soviet practices which make it advisable also to consider other hypotheses.

These practices must be placed beside the device of staging political events which serve not only as propaganda for home and foreign consumption, but probably also as ritual proof, somewhat on the order of the pleasure which a certain type of woman takes in wearing flowers which she has sent herself on a public occasion. In reply to a question about reports that peasants wrote letters to the newspapers accusing the chairman of a collective farm of being a thief, an informant said:

> No peasants write letters voluntarily. If the Party has an eye on the chairman, they go to a peasant and say: "Ivan, you know the chairman is a thief and he has to be removed. We want the whole of Russia to know about it." Then the peasant writes the letter. The whole thing is a comedy like a theatre. The term for this is *inspiratsiya.* State loans are engineered in the same way.

There are, of course, jokes about these synthetic successes. A DP informant tells about a meeting:

> The lecturer made a point that in Tsarist days ten ships a week left a certain port and now 100 did. A man from the port stood up and said it was not so; only two ships a week left the port. The lecturer was a little taken aback and then he said: "You are a fool. You do not read *Pravda."*

The trials may be seen as elaborate demonstrations that traitors existed in the Soviet Union, and that the most drastic measures were necessary to suppress such dangerous forces. Whether or not the Old Bolsheviks who actually confessed had committed any of the particular acts attributed to them was essentially irrelevant. They could be persuaded—as a service to the Party and out of their own knowledge of their political opposition, which in Party theory was itself a crime—to confess and receive punishment for a large number of crimes which they had not committed, thereby "proving" that such crimes were in fact being committed or at least plotted, and that measures must and had been taken against them.

A high NKVD official is reported to have explained his own arrest during the great Purge as follows:[38]

> The highest leadership and the People's Commissar U. . . . in particular, know my activity very well; they also know that I could not be a political criminal; and if, despite this, they have arrested me and have accused me of this and that, there are obviously weighty political grounds, and it is not the business of a small person to go against the party line; on the contrary it is necessary to help its accomplishments.

Krivitsky[39] refers to attempts to stage trials outside the Soviet Union, notably in the United States and in Czechoslovakia, which would give further verisimilitude to the charges of foreign espionage. The attempt to construct a demonstration trial in Czechoslovakia, as further described by an informant, included approaching a large number of highly placed persons, journalists, etc., and finally planting documents on a former Communist refugee from Nazi Germany after he had been denounced to the Czech police as a Nazi spy. The belief that it would be possible to stage such trials successfully even outside the

---

[38] From an unpublished manuscript by a former Soviet historian.
[39] W. G. Krivitsky, *In Stalin's Secret Service,* Harper & Brothers, New York, 1939, pp. 168–70.

Soviet Union is an example of the lengths to which the sense of their being the executors of History can lead Soviet imagination in viewing the outside world as included in the audience. The 1949 trials in Hungary, in which plotting with Tito was confessed, is a continuation, within the area of Soviet control, of the type of dramatization found in the trials in the late thirties.

Another excellent recent example of the willingness of the Party leadership to take part in a drama which to the outside world looked like a very poor fake was presented by the elections in Czechoslovakia, which had the contrived appearance of there being several political parties who were competing freely among themselves, when, actually, all the "permitted" parties had agreed in advance to join in a single bloc with the Communists and to leave to the electors a choice of voting for this single ticket or of running the risk of voting against it. Dr. David Rodnick, who was doing field work in Czechoslovakia at the time, describes the procedure as follows:[40]

> Some weeks before the so-called "election" every storekeeper was required to put in his front window a poster urging support for the unity list. In all public offices and railroad stations there were banners or placards with the words "He who loves the Republic will vote for the Republic," or "White ticket— black thoughts," and so on. It took courage for an individual to use the white voting slip in the "election" on May 30th. In almost all polling stations, the box for the white ballots was out in the open and surrounded by watchers from the local Communist Party. Each voter had been given two ballots beforehand; a red ballot which had the government list inside and a white one which was blank. Each ballot was in an envelope and could be marked at home, sealed, and brought back to the voting station. There a voter's name was checked off the list and he was permitted to go to the back of the room where the ballot boxes were theoretically supposed to be behind screens. No screens were in any of the polling stations we heard of; both boxes were out in the open. The voter was supposed to drop a ballot in either the government box or the white-ballot box, and to discard the ballot he did not use in either the waste basket for the red ballots or the one for the white ballots. As many "paper" Communist watchers told us later on, it was very difficult to get by them. They were supposed to mark down the names of all individuals who voted the white ballot and to try to intimidate them by asking them if they weren't going in the wrong direction when they approached the white ballot box. It was impossible to cast a ballot without everyone knowing how one voted. Many individuals who wished to cast a white ballot but were afraid of the consequences used their red envelope, but instead of putting in the red ballot they inserted pictures of Thomas G. Masaryk, President Benes, Jan Masaryk, Franklin D. Roosevelt, Winston Churchill, caricatures of Josef Stalin, Gottwald, Hitler, toilet paper, or nothing. Many also wrote notes attacking the Communists. Official counters from various parts of Czechoslovakia told us later on that the Ministry of Interior in Prague confiscated ballot boxes without permitting them to be

---

[40] David Rodnick, "Czechs, Slovaks, and Communism," excerpt concerning the Communist "Election" of May, 1948, taken from Chap. XVI of unpublished manuscript. See Appendix E for further details on the Czechoslovakian election.

counted, or if they had already been counted, gave out abnormally low figures. One counter in a city of 35,000 told us that in his district alone he counted 860 white ballots, and friends of his who had also served as counters in other parts of the city told him afterward that they counted as much and sometimes more than in his district. The official count for white ballots in the whole city was 216! In other parts of Czechoslovakia we were told of similar instances, where the total white ballots for a whole town or city would be given out as much smaller than had been counted in only one district.

Whereas the American commentator is concerned with the degree of manipulation, the Soviet propagandist is concerned with the appearance of complete control as the essential point.

Less spectacular, but even more revealing, are the details of the trials which are held year after year within the Soviet Union, in which the politically suspect are convicted through dramatizations of crimes which they might have committed, confessions of which are obtained by pressure and torture.

The same manuscript referred to above[41] discusses a rationale given by high officials in the secret police, called "social political prophylaxis," for the apprehension and elimination of potential criminals:

> In practice social prophylaxis presupposes as a consequence not only the apprehension of the criminal but also the establishment of criminal mood, criminal position, and criminal readiness, three degrees preceding the actual criminal act or the attempt at one. This is attained by systematic observation and study of the appropriate objects on the basis of objective signs (social origin, objective activity, relatives and personal connections, attitude toward work, etc.) with the help of secret informants. . . . After the criminal position or readiness of a certain person is established with details which do not evoke doubts—thence the conviction of the "infallibility" of the NKVD—there follows, not always, but when it is useful, an arrest. . . . The preliminary inquiry does not serve the purpose of discovering who is the real criminal since he actually has already been discovered, . . . not for the clarification of the circumstances and details of the crime *since it has not yet occurred* [italics ours] but only for the so-called "formulation" which comes down to the categorization of the potential crime according to the criminal code, putting it under the proper article and giving it all the appearance of a real action; then the court which issues the sanction (permission to hold under arrest) views the potential crime as real one.

It is furthermore of great interest that this same investigator, who had an opportunity for discussion with many high NKVD officials thoroughly familiar with all the details of "the composition of accusatory fables," could find no one who could give an answer to his question as to why all these "social fables" were necessary in order to eliminate "potential criminals." Yet the fables occur at every level on the world stage, in a satellite country, and also in remote regions of the Soviet Union. The staged trials in Bulgaria must be considered together with an informant's description of a trial—in a lower court—of a man who refused to make the required confession. Another man who looked

---

[41] See footnote 38, page 46.

like the accused was brought in to make the confession, and the accused was shot.

If we understand that these apparently different pieces of behavior—willingness to accept a report from a Machine Tractor Station that it is 100 per cent ready for Spring work although half of the tractors break down the first week, the routine handling of prisoners, and such elaborately contrived events as the great trials, the confessions in Hungary, and the Czech elections—and consider them together as instances of a willingness and a need to accept or, if necessary, to concoct proofs of what the leadership believes to be "true" if not factual, we are given more of a clue to Soviet behavior than is obtained from an attempt to explain one part of the behavior as mere inefficiency and graft and the other part as mere crude attempts to deceive.

The great religions of the world are characterized by comparable ritual representations of that which is most ardently believed, and religious wars have been fought over the degree of reality in the ritual and over how much of what was re-enacted was actually true. Those who denied the truth of the ritual were always likely to believe that the priesthoods who claimed belief were simply consciously deceiving the people. It is extremely easy to pass the same judgment on the leadership of the Soviet Union and to fail to take into account their genuine fanaticism.

The Party leadership in Russia is building, very quickly, as complete a semblance as possible of the world as they wish to see it. Production records in which the true and the hoped for are intermingled, prisoners who confess to crimes which they did not commit, lines of tractors reported "in full repair" and unable to get to the fields, voters who are forced by every possible manipulative trick to vote for the Communist Party—all these are dramatizations by and to a leadership who believe they are the custodians and executors of historical Truth.

The mechanism of belief, even in one who was fully aware of what lay behind the trials and of the accused's actual innocence of the acts to which they confessed, was described by a former member of the CPSU:

> The first time you are told that X is a traitor, you resist. But on your way home you have to build up a faith for yourself. You have to believe in something.

To brand these dramatizations as simple fakes—as many anti-Communists in Czechoslovakia did—is to throw away an opportunity to evaluate them more accurately. Rodnick reports on the Czech attitude:[42]

> No one thing that the Communists have done since their assumption of complete power in February antagonized the non-Communist Czechs and even many within the Party as much as the hypocritical building-up of an artificial public opinion that was created for the Party to manipulate as puppets. Nothing showed the megalomania of the Communist Party leadership more than this

[42] Rodnick, *op. cit.*

tendency to project its desires onto paper organizations and a synthetic public opinion—a move which assumed a lack of critical intelligence on the part of the non-Communists. It was a striking example of the amorality of the Communists who cynically assumed that by throwing words to the people, the latter would accept them as realities. The level of rationalization which this political campaign employed was one that could have appealed only to psychotic individuals. The only possible motivation was that the Communists had the power, expected to keep it, but wanted to cloak their intention with a synthetic "legality" which they assumed would satisfy the Czechs. Only the Nazis could have equalled the contempt for the dignity and common sense of the human being that the Communists displayed in their crude maneuvering. At the same time, they assumed a naïveté on the part of the outside world which would be willing to accept such an obvious hoax.

To fail to realize the possibility of loss of faith in the Party by young Communists who have taken part in these ritual rearrangements of facts would also be a mistake. But it is important to note that it was not the *falsifications* involved in the trials, as such, but the wholesale destruction of members of the Party who had been outstanding in their devotion which seems to have caused the loss of faith of highly placed Communists in the thirties. One of the problems which needs investigation is the dynamics of loss of faith today. It is possible that the great emphasis on empirical science which has been stressed in Soviet education makes it much more difficult for a young Communist, who is also an engineer, to accept these dramas without great skepticism. On the other hand, some sort of compartmentalization between science and political faith may be as possible a solution here as the *modus vivendi* which is often set up between religious faith and scientific method. The most cogent argument against this possibility is the existence of the Soviet intolerance of any compartmentalization, any reservations, any area in the personality which is not drenched in faith. Recent evidence suggests also the possibility of an emerging character structure in which absolute belief in the omniscient power, rather than in the ideals, of the Soviet system is crucial; doubt of the power of the system thus becomes a break in individual allegiance.

It is within this background—the political device of the Line, which is absolute and changing, the continuing fear of the coexistence of opposites within the personality and of the possibility that loyalty may be transformed into treachery at any moment, the struggle always to involve the personality and yet to develop functioning systems of organization, the fear that the smallest mistake may lead to catastrophe, and the tendency to accept ritual rather than actual demonstrations of a Truth—that the Soviet efforts to develop a new type of Soviet man will be discussed in this report.

Within these articles of faith and fear there is an indomitable belief in the power of the leadership to make Russians into a new kind of people, to hold in a firm mold that Russian character which they simultaneously see as so fluid, so likely to transform itself before their eyes. To the present possibility of recurrent transformation of good into evil which it is beyond their power to prevent, except by extraordinary and unremitting acts of will, they oppose the picture of a future in which all will be transformed purposefully and irreversibly.

> Each day lifts our people higher and higher. Today we are not those we were yesterday, and tomorrow we will not be those we are today. We are not the Russians we were before 1917, and Russia is not the same. We have changed and grown, together with those immense transformations which in the very root have changed the countenance of our country.[43]

---

[43] A. Zhdanov, *Report on the Magazines "Zvezda" and "Leningrad,"* Gospolitizdat (State Political Publishing House), 1946, p. 36.

Chapter 4

SOVIET IDEALS OF AUTHORITY RELATIONSHIPS

EXPECTATIONS FROM DIFFERENT LEADERSHIP LEVELS

In order to obtain a picture of the way in which the regime has looked at the question of transforming not only the social structure of Russia, but also the very nature of Russians, into the "new moral countenance of Soviet Man," it is useful to discriminate between the demands which are made upon three classes of people: (1) those who are responsible for everything; (2) those who are seen as assistants or lieutenants of those who are responsible for everything and who are also responsible for almost everything; and (3) those who are seen as acted upon, being educated, led, supervised, instructed, etc. This three-fold division is repeated again and again in Soviet official literature.

Speaking of the Party itself, Stalin said, in 1937:[44]

> How do things stand with regard to the Party? In our Party, if we have in mind its leading strata, there are about three to four thousand first rank leaders whom we would call our Party's General Staff. Then there are thirty to forty thousand middle rank leaders, who are our Party Corps of Officers. Then there are about a hundred to a hundred and fifty thousand of the lower rank Party Command Staff, who are so to speak our Party non-commissioned Officers.

Within this division, the leadership on any one of these levels is described as having, and is required to have, certain characteristics. The Leader himself is assumed to have all of the desirable characteristics—he is a model for everybody else. Whether any other leader is automatically and continuously endowed with all the ideal traits can become a subject of embarrassment, as in the recent retraction of a Chinese Communist newspaper which had quoted General Chou En-lai as saying that even Mao Tze-tung "cannot be considered faultless."[45]

> SHANGHAI, Sept. 10, '49.—The editor and the Peiping correspondent of the pro-Communist newspaper *Ta Kung Pao* apologized today for the publication on Aug. 22 of an article allegedly misrepresenting statements made in a speech by Gen. Chou En-lai, vice chairman of the Communist Revolutionary Council.

---

[44] J. Stalin, "Mastering Bolshevism," report to the 1937 Plenum of Central Committee of the CPSU, printed in *Bol'shevik*, April 1, 1937, p. 45.

[45] *The New York Times*, September 11, 1949, p. 41.

In a front page notice in the *Ta Kung Pao,* the editor, Wang Yunsheng, and the correspondent, Hsu Ying, also declared that they had been guilty of an "irresponsible attitude" in publishing a story that had not been submitted for revision in advance to "the person involved."

The newspaper's original report on General Chou's Peiping speech, which concerned "a new mode of life," quoted him as saying in part: "A man cannot be completely faultless and even Mao Tze-tung (chairman of the Chinese Community Party) cannot be considered faultless. Even Mao Tze-tung had to leave out complete portions of his works while compiling the 'selected works of Mao Tze-tung.' Should we not be more strict with ourselves and know our own shortcomings?"

Today's *Ta Kung Pao* notice stated that this was a misrepresentation of General Chou's remarks. Thus, for instance, Mr. Chou pointed out that "it is difficult to achieve perfection," the notice explained. "Even within the Communist Party of China only chairman Mao and comrade Liu Shao-chi (another top-ranking Communist) and a few other leaders have achieved the state of perfection."

The claims of perfection and faultlessness for Party leaders in other countries are bound to come into conflict with the CPSU doctrine of the inadmissibility of more than one power center within one's control area, but they provide an interesting illustration of the kind of leadership principle embraced in contemporary Soviet theory, a theory of the Party leader who has gained a perfect ability to diagnose the situation, to predict the course of History, and to develop a plan which will take maximum advantage of this situation.

The perfect models at the top of the Party, Lenin and Stalin, are to be imitated in, of course, descending degrees of perfection by all Party leaders down to the secretary of the smallest cell or the youngest Komsomol member. This newer, Stalinist belief in learning from perfect models contrasts with the earlier, Leninist belief in learning from a less perfect model who could err. Stalin, at the 13th Party Congress, in 1924, said, replying to Trotsky:[46]

"The Party," says Comrade Trotsky . . . "does not make mistakes." This is not true. The Party often errs. Il'ich taught us to teach the Party leadership by its own mistakes. If there were no mistakes in the Party there would be nothing to teach the Party with. Our task is to catch these mistakes, seek out their roots and show the Party and the working class how we erred and how we should not further repeat these errors. Without this the development of the Party would be impossible, without this formation of leaders and cadres our Party would be impossible, since they are formed and educated by their own mistakes.

But today the approved attitude stresses the perfection of the leader. Molotov speaks of Stalin's: ". . . profound knowledge of the history of nations . . . versatile experience as leader . . . ability to fathom and to discern in time the

---

[46] J. Stalin, in *Report of the 13th Congress Russian Communist Party (B) (XIII s'ezd Rossiiskoi Kommunisticheskoi Partii),* stenographic report, Moscow, March, 1924, p. 244.

strategic plans and tactics of . . . states . . . boldness and flexibility . . ."[47]
This is expressed at a popular level in Mikhailov's address at the 11th Komsomol Congress, March, 1949:[48]

> Millions of Soviet boys and girls carry in their hearts the images of the great
> creators of our Party and State, Lenin and Stalin. Millions of our youth are
> learning to live and work, to fight and win after the manner of Lenin and
> Stalin.

The letter to Stalin from the 11th Congress includes a poem:[49]

> And your life, your road, Comrade Stalin,
> Is taken as an example by all youth.

Of the Party it is said:

> The Party is a unity of will, which excludes all factions and splits in the power
> of the Party.[50]

> Not a single important political or organizational question is decided by our
> Soviet and other mass organizations without leading directives from the Party.[51]

> Comrade Kaligina said here that the Moscow organization in its own terri-
> torial unit felt daily the nearness of the leadership of the CC and of the chief
> of our Party, Stalin. I must say that we who are situated in the Donbass felt
> just as closely the concrete leadership of our struggle, of our construction, by
> the CC and Stalin.[52]

The whole system of centralized leadership is stated in the Report of the
Central Revision Commission of the VLKSM (Komsomols):[53]

> The Komsomol has come to its (Eleventh) Congress . . . rallied solidly
> (*splochennyi*), as never before, around its mother, the Communist Party;
> around the Central Committee of the VKP (B); and around the leader of the
> Bolshevist Party and the Soviet people, the Great Stalin.

As Stalin and the central organization in whose name Stalin's decisions are
phrased are to the whole of the Soviet Union, so also is each smaller leader to
those he leads. The functions of the Party Secretary at the provincial level are

[47] V. Molotov, "Stalin and Stalinist leadership," quoted from *Pravda*, December 21,
1949, p. 3, in *Current Digest of the Soviet Press*, Vol. 1, No. 52, January 24, 1950, p. 8.
[48] Mikhailov addressing the 11th Congress of the VLKSM, *Komsomol'skaia Pravda*,
March 31, 1949, p. 3.
[49] From a poem quoted in the 11th Congress' letter to Stalin, in *Komsomol'skaia
Pravda*, April 10, 1949, p. 1.
[50] J. Stalin, "Foundations of Leninism" (*Osnovi Leninizma*), as in Stalin, *Leninism*,
New York, 1928.
[51] *Ibid.*
[52] Sarkisov, 17th Congress of the All-Union Communist Party (B), (*XVII s'ezd
Vsesoyuznoi Kommunisticheskoi Partii*), stenographic account, Moscow, 1934, p. 161.
[53] Krivtsov, "Report of the Central Revisory Commission," *Komsomol'skaia Pravda*,
March 31, 1949, p. 4.

therefore described as follows:[54]

> . . . to know the plants exactly, to visit them regularly, to be directly in contact with the plant managers and the corresponding People's Commissariat, to support them in fulfilling the Party's plans and decisions concerning industry and transportation, to control systematically the fulfillment of those decisions, to reveal the defects in the work of the plants and to aim at their removal.

In other words, the Party secretary is to be all-knowing, all-directing. Examples of appropriate behavior for Party activists are sometimes published as models in which each step in the problem of inspiring a group is outlined.[55] Similarly, Komsomol leaders "must show to all youth an example of the socialist attitude,"[56] "set the example for all students,"[57] and young Pioneer leaders are still charged with the task of being "models of honesty, idealism, and industriousness."[58] But while each leader, no matter how humble or how young, is acting as a model for those who know less than he, all, from the lowest leader up, look all the way to the top for their models. Although there is continual exhortation to be a model, the complementary instruction to youth, to the average member of a collective farm committee, or to a factory committee is to look to Stalin and Lenin, not to the Komsomol leader or to the Party secretary in the farm or the factory.

There is a rigid realistic demand for subordination of one level of the Party to another, in which each higher level enforces its will upon the lower in the name of the Party, but this is not accompanied by a demand for personal loyalty or friendship. All such personal relations are stigmatized as "family relations." This organizational ethic provides a weak basis for organization because it includes no ties of loyalty, either from local units to local leaders or from local leaders to district or provincial leaders. There is no dogma to support any person-to-person relations of leadership and followership. Each leader is confronted with the impossible task of being a model for those who look over his head to a model higher and more perfect than he, although he is wholly accountable for them.

The implications of this peculiar leadership structure can be visualized if one imagines an army organized in such a manner that each officer is completely responsible for and accountable in regard to all those under him, both officers and men, but whose subordinates are expected to keep their eyes only on the leads given by the Commander-in-Chief as a model of perfection. Meanwhile

---

[54] *Pravda,* February 19, 1941, p. 5.

[55] See Appendix F.

[56] Rules of the Komsomol, in *Rezoliutsii i Dokumenty XI s'ezda VLKSM*, pp. 51–52.

[57] From 11th Congress' resolution "On the Work of the Komsomol in the Schools," in *Rezoliutsii i Dokumenty XI s'ezda VLKSM*, p. 28.

[58] From speech to the 11th Congress by a Komsomol member who was serving as Pioneer-leader, in *Komsomol'skaia Pravda,* April 3, 1949, p. 2.

the fact that Party officials at each level are accountable for the acts of those at lower levels stimulates the arbitrary exercise of power by all those in authority, always in the name of the Party. This makes it possible for members of each echelon within the hierarchy to see the *next* highest echelon as behaving bureaucratically; and this, in turn, may be one reason for the kind of betrayals which occur when men lose their belief in the Party.

This same demand that each individual who is responsible for others should play a model-setting role is extended to parents, who are, however, accorded much more explicit rights to direct obedience and affection from their children. While there seems to be no requirement to love a Komsomol leader or a Party secretary, affection for parents is enjoined upon children and "sons know that the love of a Soviet mother is not all-forgiving love but is exacting and proud, demanding responsibility *to her* for conduct and deeds."[59] In this respect, parents in regard to children bear a closer resemblance to Stalin's relationship to every Soviet citizen, as their right to receive love and respect is as explicitly stated as is their duty to deserve it; "Fortunately, in the majority of Soviet families, between father and children exist the very best of relations based on mutual love, respect and understanding. For the authority of the parents to be really high, a strong, well-knit family is necessary first of all. . . . If the parents are socially valuable persons and honest workers, if they share with their children their achievements at work, recount the life of their collective and events in the country, their authority will always be high in the children's eyes. . . ."[60]

Nor is any time limit put on the responsibility of parents for children or of children to parents. In a model of an exemplary family, a Soviet mother is made to say: "All the children obey me. My eldest son, who returned from the front a lieutenant, will do nothing without asking my advice, will go nowhere without having told me."[61]

This use of individual examples is one further aspect of model-setting in which a model mother, a model collective farmer, a model worker are described for the whole Soviet Union. The emphasis is on the way in which a given individual discharged a particular role, not on the individual himself. This stress on a role, illustrated by the behavior of someone half the country away, is again an interesting way in which personal loyalty to individual teachers and managers can be muted into impersonal idealism. American observers comment upon the fantastic quality of these models, the description of the perfect agitator or of the perfect collective farm. However, they will seem less fantastic

---

[59] A. Sergeyeva, "Love and Obligation to a Mother," *Family and School (Sem'ya i Shkola)*, November, 1947.

[60] N. Udina, "Parental Authority," *Family and School (Sem'ya i Shkola)*, 1946, Nos. 4–5.

[61] A. Alekseyev and M. Andreyeva, "Report of a Working Mother," *Family and School (Sem'ya i Shkola)*, April, 1948.

if understood as manifestations of the perfection already attained in vision by the Leader rather than as if they were intended to be taken as real descriptions of sober facts.

The direction of all eyes toward the top makes it possible to block out a line of spiritual ambition not unlike that available in those religions without a priesthood (a characteristic of Russian sects), in which each true believer can approach nearer and nearer to perfection. It appears probable that this insistence on the possibilities of becoming a better and better Communist, better imbued with an understanding of Marxism-Leninism, may play an important part in persuading men to assume the dangers of any sort of conspicuous role in the Soviet Union. It must, of course, be realized that there are great material rewards available to those who are able to rise, that it is difficult to refuse advancement when it is offered, and that behavior which is necessary to enable one to maintain any position on the advancement ladder is very similar to the kind of behavior which will single one out for promotion. Nevertheless, and in spite of the decrease in the danger of actual physical liquidation (after this danger to those in leadership roles had reached such a height in the late thirties that it endangered the entire trained Party leadership), it seems necessary to account further for the existence of this willingness. It is possible also that, as the latitude allowed to individual thought and initiative narrows, it is even more necessary to explain at least why men of very mediocre ability, picked out by the Party leadership as safe and reliable, are willing to run the risk of exercising their so inconsiderable talents. But the persistent propagation of the double doctrine—that it is possible to grow in the right to leadership, and that those who are purged or demoted failed to guard against some heresy—contributes to making it possible for a man who rises in the apparatus to believe, despite such overwhelming evidence to the contrary, that he will succeed. (This would be in a way comparable to the persistent American belief in success, which is held by millions of men whose real chances of making more than two or three thousand a year can be demonstrated, statistically and by their own everyday experience, as being almost nonexistent. But because, in the United States, success is believed to be "making good," to be the reward of hard work and effort, each man who strives may believe that, statistics to the contrary, he will fulfill the Horatio Alger story, he will succeed where his fellows fail.)

It is suggested that the belief that those who failed deserved to fail plays a comparable role in the lives of those who are willing to assume office in Soviet society. There is considerable evidence that, in Nazi Germany, office attracted individuals who had unusually strong desires to bully, to hurt, to torture, to control the lives of others, for the sake of the pleasure that it gave them. Thus the revelation of the Nuremberg Trials and other studies of Nazism give us a picture of administration which drew disproportionately upon the power-seeking, ruthless, cruelty-loving element in the population. If we look only at the outward political structure of the Soviet Union, with its increasing monolithic character and the great rewards in power over the lives of others which are offered to those who are able so to manipulate the power situation as to rise to the top and to stay there, we might be tempted to expect that the same personality type would obtain in the upper bureaucracy of the Soviet Union as in Nazi Germany. All material which makes it possible better to assay in more concrete detail the theories by which given men justify their attempt to reach and keep positions of power and influence in the Soviet Union assumes significance. It is also necessary to realize that the man who reaches a position of great influence and importance in the belief that he has done so because of his superior understanding and application of the principles of Marxism-Leninism rather than from a sheer openly expressed belief in the right of the stronger to dominate the weaker will not be the less ruthless in exercising the power. He may be much more ruthless, because his conscience will be entirely on his side; he will not be subject to the sort of moral collapse shown by some of the top Nazis when faced with the expression of contempt for their ideas of power by representatives of nations which had proved themselves more powerful than they. The Soviet leader seems to be of a different caliber and subject to very different sorts of pressures. His own failure may convince him that *he* was wrong but not that the political faith in which he believed was wrong. His own failure, his demotion or liquidation by his own Party, may serve merely as a reinforcement of his belief in his Party's rightness.

It is in this way that contemporary Soviet literature portrays the Communist who is exposed and demoted. So Tverdova (in Virta's play, *Our Daily Bread*[62]), chairman of the executive committee in a small locality, who has been a Communist for many years and is an experienced and able administrator, is "unmasked" by the new Party secretary. She first exclaims:

> Twenty years I spent for this cause and now I am politically bankrupt, shaken out of the calesh.

Then after a pause, she continues:

> And so what! In what I am guilty I will render account, looking straight. I have to think it all over, I have to think hard.

This attitude, expressed in a 1947 play, continues that dramatized in the great trials. At the January, 1937, trial Radek discussed his misgivings concerning the First Five-Year Plan:[63]

---

[62] N. Virta, *Our Daily Bread* (*Khleb nash nasushchnyi*), *Zvezda* (*The Star*), June, 1947.

[63] Radek, Report of Court Proceedings in the Case of the Anti-Trotskyite Centre, heard before the Military Collegium of the Supreme Court of the USSR, Moscow, January 23–30, 1937. Published by the People's Commissariat of Justice of the USSR, Moscow, 1937, p. 84–85.

Already . . . in 1931 . . . I thought it was necessary to hold back the economic offensive. . . . I dissented on the main question: on the question of continuing . . . the Five-Year Plan. To analyze these disagreements from the Social angle— of course, I then believed the tactics which I regarded as correct to be the best Communist tactics— . . . history's joke was that I overestimated the power of resistance . . . of . . . the Kulaks . . . (and) of the middle peasants to pursue an independent policy. I was scared by the difficulties and thus became a mouth-piece of . . . forces hostile to the proletariat.

This hypothesis, that the discipline of others is believed to have been de-served and that one's own discipline is accepted as a proof of uncorrectness, would provide an additional explanation of the way in which those who have been disciplined, demoted, or banished go to work again with apparent zeal, apart from the calculus of external rewards and punishment.

CHARACTERISTICS OF THE IDEAL LEADER

We may now consider the way top leadership is officially said to gain and maintain its superior capacity to lead. Materials on this subject come from a variety of sources—the statements of Lenin and Stalin to the Party, the continual admonishment and exhortation in the Party press, exhortation to Komsomol and pioneer leaders, and the popular pictures of the leadership presented to the average citizen and to children. These will be considered together, since they may all be regarded as officially inspired, although the details may differ as to whether Stalin is presented in a synthetic folk song as the direct descendant of the Bogatyri, to the educators as the Perfect Educator, to the Literary Front as the master of organization of literary activity, etc. The basic intent, the virtues emphasized are fundamentally the same, and their reappearance in different forms should serve as reinforcement of faith in the dogma of the regime. (There are very few data available on the degree to which the beliefs of the top leadership about their own roles differ from the beliefs considered suitable for the masses of the people. What little evidence there is suggests that the difference lies not so much in the actual belief, in, for example, the superior capacity of Stalin to lead the Soviet Union, as in the tone of the belief. To the populace he may be presented as a loving, kind leader, to the inner circle of the elite he may appear as being much more interested in personal power, yet to both he will be *the* Leader, with any present alternative regarded as impossible. That is, the chain of reasoning which forms the con-nection between the Leadership and History may be quite different, but the belief in the absolute connection may nevertheless be there. The same informant who will relate a gossipy report in inner circles that Stalin decided on the Line first and then said, "Let the theoreticians justify it," will also report on Stalin's stubborn fidelity to his view of Leninism, and Stalin's personal fanatical de-votion to building a state which will stand after his death.)

In tracing the details of this leadership role, it will be useful to consider

Lenin and Leninist Marxism as given in the sense that the original founding prophet and the scriptures might be present in any ongoing religious system. World History as it is presented to the young citizen of the Soviet Union is divided in two: before 1917 and after 1917. After 1917, the picture is of an all-embracing way of life, with a Truth, a form of organization (the Party), the embodiment of that organizational form in a leader (Lenin and Stalin), and a way of life—difficult, all demanding—to which every Soviet citizen should feel called, to at least some degree, as a vocation. In these respects it is far closer to the familiar picture of a religious movement in its early, all-inclusive form than to the sort of political picture presented by contemporary Western democracies.

Some of the most vivid material on the leader comes from the large amount of folklore which was developed during the late twenties and early thirties and in which Lenin and Stalin were fitted into poetic forms of Great Russia, the *byliny,* and into the folklore forms of some of the non-Russian peoples of Asia. These poems were published with the specific statement that they represented spontaneous outpourings of the common people who had adapted the new Bolshevik figures to their idiom. They are quoted here as evidence of what it is considered desirable for the people to think.

In the folklore the people are pictured as gathering together, "from the old to the middle ones, from the middle ones to the young ones, and asking 'Who should be ruling?' " And they all "spoke the same speech," they all chose one "Vladimir Il'ich, the Leader Lenin," and they "entrusted all of Russia to him, to the leader Lenin and his helper, with the entire Bolshevik Party." Another revision of an old folktale, about three brothers searching for Truth, tells how one went to the factory "to seek for Truth," for "there you will find out more rapidly what it is. You hold it in your hand." And "Lenin's Truth" found in the factory "went over the whole world. . . . And in October of the seventeenth year, the Truth announced itself, started to speak in a loud voice and ring over the entire world." "The workers and peasants went to war, 'And Lenin himself was leading them, together with his helper Stalin. . . . And Lenin's Truth gained the upper hand' and from then on the people are not 'hunched over . . . they do not water the earth with their tears—they are the owners of their factories, their earth, and their lives.' "

Stalin appears in the folklore as the direct successor of Lenin, as his helper during life, who derived his relations to the Truth directly from contact with Lenin. The folklore celebrates the occasion when Stalin is pictured as coming to join Lenin in exile, and Krupskaya, wife of Lenin, says: "Look out of the window, Il'ich, isn't that Stalin, glorious hero?" The story of Stalin's acceptance of Lenin's Testament is told: "The entire earth was wet with tears. Our hero —Stalin-light—took off his cap from his saddened head, and he spoke to the people, thus 'We are laying down an oath for eternity. . . . We are laying down an oath that we shall carry out things as you wanted it. With your wisdom we shall live. . . . Goodbye Il'ich, sleep quietly.' "

A long saga asks the question: "Who is like Lenin, in mind and powerful force?" and answers "Stalin," who "held in his powerful hand" the "golden sun": "He is great and wise like Lenin. . . . He is the same as Lenin, friendly and good." . . . "Together with the Sun the Great Stalin brought to our tents the belief in our own strength. He is great and simple, like Lenin."

In the approved poetry of the new folklore, as in the continued repetition of the names of Lenin and Stalin and in the phrase Leninism-Stalinism, the halo around the figure of Lenin is made to embrace Stalin also, and he, like Lenin, in obedience to Lenin, sharing Lenin's knowledge of the Truth, leads the people, will "give happiness to all the people." But at the same time the relationship of every Soviet citizen to the leader is stressed. "All have in their blood a drop of Lenin's blood," says a long poem, written sometime in the early thirties, and "We have become terrible for enemies as Lenin himself." This same theme appears in a postwar novel, *The Stozharovs*,[64] in which a young army officer, still in his teens, says: ". . . Stalin, he knows, and that is why he is so sure of the people, of our victory and of everything. . . . It seems to me . . . that in each Communist there is a kind of particle of Stalin. In any true Communist, of course. And this helps him to be sure and calm, to know what to do, to what everything will lead if he acts as the Party commands . . . a Communist . . . he is a leader in everything and everywhere, a teacher of life for the people."

Throughout the folklore, as in the Party histories, the plot is the search for the Truth, for the power which in the folklore is represented as the ring which, when grasped, will turn the whole world over. Lenin found it and Stalin carries on the tradition. In a recent Soviet poem[65] in the form of a lullaby, in which a father bids his baby daughter sleep safely now that atomic energy has been found, this figure recurs—of a granite mountain, "which is barring our way. Long, long ago it should have been turned upside down, long, long ago it should have been forced to give up its ore, and now at the prearranged hour . . . the old mountain disappeared."

So we have an emphasis on the ideal leader's undeviating, absolute following of the Truth which Lenin found and from this Truth obtaining his power. Application of the Truth is expressed in foresight and long sight, and, in the folklore, this wide yet focused view is symbolized by placing in Stalin's hand a spyglass as he stands on the walls of the Kremlin, as he "looks and rules the country solicitously, he looks and looks without ever getting tired. His sensitive ear hears everything, his sharp glance sees everything; how the people live, how

[64] Elena Katerli, *The Stozharovs*, 1948, pp. 147–49 and p. 169.
[65] See Appendix G.

they work." This combination of wide perspective and power to direct is expressed of Lenin as follows: "Lifting his head higher than the stars, Lenin could see at once the entire world and he could direct the entire world at one time."

Again this same behavior is urged on the local leader, so a regional Party secretary moralizes in a recent novel, *In Some Populated Place*,[66] speaking of life in the country: "Our influence must express itself in all spheres. . . . We know and understand that we must go deeper into the life of the Party organization. . . . We will go forward only by seeing wider than one division, by seeing further than the present day. We must lead the whole life of the *raion*." And this same Party secretary is described as "the brains and soul of the *raion* . . . walking idly among the crowd to listen to what the people are thinking."

These two aspects of leadership, the top leader who sees all without moving from his place on the Kremlin wall, the lower leader who combines his wider vision with a closer knowledge of the people, are summed up in the plot of a recent Soviet film, *The Train Goes East*, in which the heroine, a Communist girl, is delayed on a railway platform together with a great many other people. She first mingles with the people, learning all about them, and then, when the train dispatcher loses his voice, mounts to the traffic control tower and directs the people, about whom she now knows everything, absolutely correctly to their particular trains.

The Soviet critic is exhorted to "illuminate with a searchlight the road to tomorrow,"[67] and the criticism which surrounded the hero of a favorite juvenile war tale, *Timur*, first condemned the character of Timur as having been just "thought up," but later the condemnation was retracted and it was recognized that the author, in a novel, "saw the boy of the future," "he discerned the tendency of development of the Soviet child such as he would be tomorrow,"[68] and a wife rebukes her husband, who questions a decision of local leaders: "You may argue how you like but . . . 'they' are right, they see farther than we do."[69]

With this emphasis on all-seeingness, on a focused vision and a power of diagnosis which is wider and deeper than that of those who are led, goes a requirement to focus action, to go indeflectibly, though sometimes circuitously, toward the goal, and always to have perfect timing, being neither too early, which is Left, nor too late, which is Right. Stalin says: "It is the function of

[66] Boris Galin, "In Some Populated Place" (*v odnom naselennom punkte*), *Novyi Mir*, November, 1947.

[67] From the report of Andrei Zhdanov about the literary magazines *Zvezda* and *Leningrad*, published in *Literaturnaya Gazeta*, September 21, 1946.

[68] L. Kon, "The Educational Significance of the Works of Arkadii Gaidar," *Literature in School* (*Literatura v shkole*), April, 1948.

[69] S. Babyevski, "The Cavalier of the Golden Star" (*Kavaler zolotoi zvezdy*), published in *Oktyabr'*, April, 1947, p. 56.

Leninist theory to diagnose the situation at the moment and thus determine the direction of the blow and to focus it on a proper line through the organization of revolutionary forces."[70] The Komsomol is described as organized and disciplined, firm, purposeful, and persistent in everything he undertakes. He should walk a narrow path to his goal without stopping, without swerving.

When we look at the history of the condemnation of the Right and Left deviations, as demonstrated in the late twenties and early thirties, we find the same emphasis on the need for steering a course between twin dangers. Stalin has given us graphic descriptions of both.

In a 1930 statement about the Rights, he says:[71]

> They are suffering from the same disease as . . . that . . . hero of Chekhov, the man in the leather case. Do you remember Chekhov's story titled *The Man in the Leather Case?* That he always went about in galoshes and wadded coat, with an umbrella, both in hot and cold weather? . . . "Why do you need galoshes and a wadded coat in July? . . ." Belikov used to be asked.

> "You never know," Belikov replied, "what if something happens? There might be a sudden frost; what should I do then?" . . . A new restaurant was opened, and Belikov was . . . in alarm: "It might, of course, be a good thing to have a restaurant, but take care, see that nothing happens." . . . Do you remember the affair of the technical colleges being transferred to the Economic People's Commissariats? We wanted to hand over only two technical colleges to the Supreme Economic Council. A small matter it might seem. Yet we met with the most desperate resistance on the part of the Right deviators. "Hand over two technical colleges to the SEC? Why? Hadn't we better wait? Take care, see that nothing happens as a result of this scheme. . . ." Or, for example, the question of the emergency measures against the kulaks. "Do you remember what hysterics the leaders of the Right opposition fell into on this occasion? . . . Take care, see that nothing happens as a result of this scheme." Yet today we are applying the policy of liquidating the kulaks as a class, a policy in comparison with which the extraordinary measures against the kulaks are a mere fleabite.

In his political report of June 27, 1930, to the Central Committee of the 16th Congress,[72] Stalin discusses both the Left exaggeration (*peregib*) and the Right overestimation of the severity of the temporary setbacks to and arrests of the current offensive:

> . . . (some) think that the socialist offensive is a headlong march forward . . . without regrouping of forces in the course of the offensive, without consolidating the positions occupied, without utilizing reserves to develop our successes, and, if symptoms have appeared of, say, an ebb of a part of the peasantry away from the collective farms, this means . . . a check to the offensive. Is this true?

---

[70] J. Stalin, Political Report of the Central Committee of the 16th Congress of the Communist Party of the Soviet Union, in *Leninism,* Vol. 2, New York, 1933, pp. 414–15.

[71] *Ibid.*

[72] J. Stalin, Political Report of the Central Committee to the 16th Congress of the Communist Party of the Soviet Union, in *Leninism,* Vol. 2, New York, 1933.

> Of course it is untrue. In the first place, not a single offensive . . . takes place
> without some breaks and over-hastiness on individual sections of the front. . . .
> Secondly, there never has been, and never can be, a *successful* offensive without
> a regrouping of forces in the course of the offensive itself, without consolidat-
> ing the occupied positions, without utilizing reserve. . . . In a headlong move-
> ment, i.e., one that does not observe these conditions, the offensive must in-
> evitably work itself to a standstill and collapse. Rushing forward headlong is
> fatal in an offensive. Our rich experience in our civil war teaches us this.

The Left deviation represents uncontrolled, romantic, not properly calculated
behavior; and the Right, spineless pessimism and a tendency to surrender easily
before setbacks or obstacles.

But the Bolshevik leader must remain indeflectable, calm; he must be particularly wary against the seductions of the path of least resistance, of being
seduced, without knowing it, into becoming a tool of the enemy forces. "Lenin
said, 'The honest opportunities are the most dangerous,' " warns the new party
secretary who is unmasking the old secretary.[73]

In the same political report[74] in which Stalin satirized the Rights, he also
said:

> In our party there are some who think that we ought not to have called a
> halt to the Left exaggerators. They think that we ought not to have offended
> our workers and counteracted their excitement, even if this excitement led to
> mistakes. . . . Only those who want at all costs to swim with the stream can
> say that. They are the very same people who will never learn the Leninist
> policy of going against the stream when . . . the interests of the Party demand
> it. They are tailists and not Leninists.

The young Komsomol is warned against being *respushchenyi, raskhlyabanyi,*
and *razboltanyi,* words which together carry connotations of being lax, loose,
relaxed and slovenly, untied, hanging loosely, and of talking too much.

But the virtues of proceeding firmly to overcome obstacles are of no use in
themselves. They are only recognized when placed at the service of Party goals.
A writer who apparently was taking the right course, i.e., "choosing historical
themes,"[75] is condemned because his intent was corrupted by his choice of "the
way of least resistance." Nor is it permissible for a Communist to choose a
difficult task for the sheer enjoyment of struggle. The young hero of the
Soviet film, *Secret Mission,* exclaims with delight when he is told by his Party
superior about the dangerous German adversary with whom he is to match wits
abroad. He is immediately rebuked for expressing any such preference; it would
have been better for the cause "had he (the adversary) been weak." But of a

---

[73] N. Virta, "Our Daily Bread" (*Khleb nash nasushchnyi*), *Zvezda,* June, 1947, p. 47.

[74] J. Stalin, Political Report of the Central Committee to the 16th Congress of the
Communist Party of the Soviet Union, in *Leninism,* Vol. 2, New York, 1933.

[75] Sofronov, criticizing the play of N. Pogodin, *The Bygone Years* (*Minuvshiye
gody*), in *Oktyabr',* February, 1949, p. 142.

favorably characterized Communist in a recent novel,[76] it is said, "He has become so familiar with the conception of the vanguard role of Communists that he cannot swim merely with the current of events," which he himself describes as "lagging behind."

The combined demands on perspective, puritanism, and refusal to swim with the current may all occur together, as in the comment by Stalin[77] that "this deficiency consists in the desire of a number of our comrades to swim with the current smoothly and peacefully, without pespective, without looking into the future, so that all around there is a festive and holiday feeling."

Moving against the current is, of course, one way of maintaining the iron control which is also demanded of a Bolshevik. A heroine struggling with the moral problems facing Soviet youth is made to say of herself:[78] "Disgraceful! . . . I have no character, no self-control, no real will. I fly down a slope and cannot check myself." In a much-discussed postwar novel, *Comrade Anna,*[79] the heroine, nearly going out of her mind from grief, considers shooting herself but is stopped by the thought of her child. This scene is omitted from later editions of the novel as being out of character for a positive Soviet heroine. (In this connection it is worth noting that women do not appear, except as the most casual mention includes men and women, in the official folklore as it refers to Stalin. Lenin is represented with his wife, but Stalin holds the sun in one hand and the moon—a feminine symbol in the old folklore—in the other and is credited with a long list of fructifying deeds: "Where he stepped, a trace remained, each step a new town, a bridge, a railroad . . . towns, houses, like cliffs; over the entire earth he sowed things that are stronger than granite." However, in the novels and plays, women appear in the lower ranks of the Party, faced with the same moral struggles as men in addition to the particular complications incident to their sex, so that material on female Party members at this level seems as valid as material on male Party members.)

With this requirement, that all behavior be controlled and directed toward Party goals, goes the requirement that the Party member treat himself as a tool to carry out the wishes of the Party, but that he be at all times a conscious tool, voluntarily submitting himself to the discipline of the Party. And the discipline must be minute and detailed, over himself and over his every movement. So an informant reports an encounter with a Soviet professor in Berlin, who told her that he smoked a pipe, "because while smoking a pipe the face does not reveal so much." Then he added:

See, this we learned during the Soviet period. Before the revolution we used

[76] Bubyonnov, "The White Birch," *Oktyabr,'* July, 1947, p. 24.
[77] Excerpt from Stalin's report at 15th Party Congress, 1927.
[78] Elena Il'ina, *Fourth Height* (*Chetvertaya vysota*), Detgiz, 1948.
[79] Antonina Koptyayeva, "Comrade Anna" (*Tovarishch Anna*), in *Oktyabr'*, May, 1946, p. 97.

to say: "The eyes are the mirror of the soul." The eyes can lie—and how. You can express with your eyes a devoted attention which in reality you are not feeling. You can express serenity or surprise. It is much more difficult to govern the expression of your mouth. I often watch my face in the mirror before going to meetings and demonstrations and I saw. . . . I was suddenly aware that even with a memory of a disappointment my lips became closed. That is why by smoking a heavy pipe you are more sure of yourself. Through the heaviness of the pipe the lips are deformed and cannot react spontaneously.

This quotation is a virtual diagram of the shift from the old pre-Soviet type of interpersonal relationship to the new: In the old, dissimulation is a pretense of positive feeling; in the new, it is a hiding of negative feeling. Contrasts such as this occur frequently in the course of the Bolshevik attempt to impose rigid controlled focus on a people whose habitual behavior had been diffuse, expressive, and less controlled. Echoes of the way in which the standard Bolshevik behavior is reflected among those who are opposed to the regime are found in the words of a recent émigré:[80] "We (the opposed) recognize each other at once by looking at the eyes, at the scarcely noticeable smiles, by the way such a man greets a Party member. He says: Hello, friendly. We recognize none the less, that he belongs to us. We recognize such a man by the way he sits at a general meeting, and also by the way he listens. But we consider it good manners to avoid personal acquaintance."

Both of these quotations throw some light on why the Party likes to have meetings, which often appear like mere mechanical rubber stamping of official policy; among other things, they provide an opportunity for watching for these tell-tale signs.

The Party member must never relax, never look for rest or for the good things of this world. "Our generation is not born to have a rest."[81]

Immediately after the war, there was added, to this demand for unrelaxed alertness, a positive stress on restlessness (*bespokoistvo*) which was illustrated in fiction by stories of the good Communists who returned from the front to find their own communities apathetic and self-satisfied. The restless veteran then became a leader who turned the local community upside down. Approval of restlessness was used as a prod to those who thought "after the victory will come a respite, that one would be able to work now with less than full strength," but this was castigated; people must work now "with active Bolshevik restlessness."[82] In late 1949 this stress on restlessness has disappeared;

---

[80] N. Osipov, "Immigration Inside the USSR," *Grani,* Issue 5, Hanau, Germany, July–August, 1949.

[81] K. Simonov, "Under the Chestnut Trees of Prague," *Znamya,* February–March, 1946.

[82] S. Babayevski, "The Cavalier of the Golden Star" (*Kavaler zolotoi svezdi*), *Oktyabr',* April, 1947.

whether this is because there is too much real restlessness to be directed into useful channels or because the veteran has become such a commonplace that he no longer provides a useful model it is impossible to tell. This ephemeral choice of a virtue for Party members, in terms of a special situation, and its later neglect is an example of the extreme contemporaneousness which, in the Soviet Union, accompanies the attempt to politicize every act and every mood.

Another extremely important characteristic of the Party leader, at all levels, is watchfulness (*bditel'nost'*), which entails being continuously alert toward the self and toward others for the slightest signs of doubt or of slackening of effort, with the expected sequels: treachery and penetration by the enemy. "The enemies are not asleep," says an editorial in *Molodoi Bol'shevik*, "They use any sliver in order to create inside the country points of support for anti-Soviet propaganda."[83] But because this is so, watchfulness includes watchfulness over one's closest friends: "true friendship and comradely care do not exclude but, on the contrary, presuppose the highest demands, the sharpest and most merciless criticism."[84] This demand, in an editorial in 1948, is a repetition, on a more routine scale, of the demand which accompanied the purge period in the thirties, that one's best friends be sacrificed to the Party. The leadership is surrounded by enemies, "walking as a small closed group on a steep and difficult road with solidly joined hands . . . surrounded on all sides by enemies, they have to walk almost under their fire."[85] And always this enemy may be quite close to one. In contemporary novels, the upper Party man who proves to be dangerous to the well-being of the Party now is pictured as having many misleading good qualities. Today he is pictured as a large man, whereas fifteen years ago he was puny.[86] He is sympathetic, one of the group, not a stranger. His relationship with his family is good.[87] He is represented as strong and with strong convictions.[88] Under such circumstances the good Party leader has to be doubly watchful. "It is not enough," warns Sofronov,[89] "to pay attention to what is said, which may be quite in accord with the Party program, but one must pay attention to the tone, to the love with which a school teacher may quote the poems which are criticized in the (official) school program. The same thing may be said about the critics and the pleasure with which they cite the plays which they condemn." And suspicion of vague, unrecognizable,

[83] Editorial, "Education Soviet Patriotism—the Most Important Task of the Komsomol," *Molodoi Bol'shevik,* September, 1947.

[84] Editorial, "Care for the friend—a Komsomol duty," *Komsomol'skaia Pravda,* August 6, 1948, p. 1.

[85] Quotation from Lenin in V. Ozerov, "The Image of a Bolshevik," *Bol'shevik,* Issue 10, May, 1949.

[86] Y. Olesha, *Envy,* Moscow, 1927.

[87] K. Simonov, "Smoke of the Fatherland," *Novyi Mir,* November, 1947.

[88] *Ibid.*

[89] Sofronov, "About Soviet Dramaturgy," *Oktyabr',* February, 1949.

inimical atmospheres is maintained by such statements as that of the Soviet writer, Perventsev,[90] who told an audience that "soon after the war was over" the theatrical market in the Soviet Union was inundated with "inscrutable speed" by foreign plays. This watchfulness for the enemy which lurks behind the most friendly façade is summed up in the play *Under the Chestnut Trees of Prague*,[91] when Petrov says to Masha, who has seen Prague:

> So you rode through the city, you saw people walking in the streets; these people seem to be more or less the same and everybody wears more or less the same hats, more or less the same glasses and gloves. But behind which glasses are hidden the eyes of a Fascist? Under which hat is the head secretly thinking about how everything could be turned back? In which gloves are the hands which would like to strangle us all with pleasure? All this you have not seen?

Every Party leader must reckon with the fact that "one of the most important results of oppositionist work . . . is that it is used by a third force, outside the walls of the Party, which says it is not important to me who you are, but you are the enemy of my enemy; therefore you are my friend."[92]

The need for eternal watchfulness is enhanced by the Bolshevik refusal to admit that anything is accidental. As Lominadze says in his new pledge of adherence at the 17th Party Congress:[93]

> I must begin with the fact that the mistakes which brought me to the opposition were not accidental. People do not start on the opportunist path accidentally. Accidental opposition cannot exist in the Party.

The appropriate behavior for the Party leadership faced with such grave dangers within and without is to watch over everything and control everything. This demand for total responsibility, total control is reiterated again and again and has been discussed above (see page 60) in the image of the all-seeingness, all-directingness of the leader.

At the same time, however, that these demands for total control and rigid discipline are made on the leaders, the image of the leader is presented popularly as one who leads through closeness to the people, using inspiration and persuasion rather than physical force. We have noted the discrepancy in the Soviet theory of leadership, which enjoins each Party member to be a model for those beneath him but which, instead of enjoining those below to model themselves reciprocally on their immediate superiors, enjoins all Party members

---

[90] A. Perventsev, speech at Plenum Session, Board of All-Soviet Writers, *Oktyabr'*, February, 1949.

[91] K. Simonov, "Under the Chestnut Trees of Prague," *Znamya*, February–March, 1946.

[92] M. P. Tomsky, 16th Congress of the All-Union Communist Party (B) (*XVI s'ezd Vsesoyuznoi Kommunisticheskoi Partii*), stenographic account, Moscow, 1931, p. 145.

[93] Lominadze, 17th Congress of the All-Union Communist Party (B) (*XVII s'ezd Vsesoyuznoi Kommunisticheskoi Partii*), stenographic account, Moscow, 1934, p. 118.

of whatever level to model themselves on the top leaders, Lenin and Stalin. A second discrepancy can be found in the theory which alerts every leader to the need to control everything, as the slightest error may lead to total disaster (which is a virtual injunction to lead by harsh controls and force), and a theory of leadership, presented to those who are to be led, which represents the leader as friendly, happiness-giving, and approachable. In the folklore Stalin is thus "the leader and friend of all the people." The picture of the leader who leads by a focused vision which directs his people rather than by force is presented in the folklore picture in which the leader holds his spyglass in his right hand and the reins of his horse in his left, while the Don Cossack holds, in his right hand, a sword.

The images which stress the leader's patience, understanding, humaneness, power to awaken and sustain enthusiasm, are a source of continual confusion in the admonitions and models presented to Party members. There is no room in this picture for any physical force used against one's own people. "Lenin will be remembered in a different way. He sowed light once more where Nikolai made darkness . . . alone, in eight years he built what they had destroyed in a thousand years." And when asked about Lenin, the people answered, "he is the son of his own people, immensely powerful . . . and the peoples surrounded Lenin even closer, like a flock of swallows." And of Stalin the folklore says:

> Where Joseph light walks
> There a spring will come to the surface
> A spring will rise, grass will grow,
> Grass grows, flowers bloom,
> The working people loved Joseph light.

In the Soviet propaganda film *Alexander Nevsky*, celebrating the medieval Russian hero, the conqueror-leader rides bareheaded into the city, catching up children into his arms to ride with him, and his soldiers do the same. In the same film, the conqueror releases the vassals of the German attackers, who are pictured as fighting involuntarily, and holds the leaders for ransom, and it is only the Russian traitor who has helped the Germans who is destroyed—by the people, not by decree of the leaders. In a recent Soviet newsreel showing the 1949 May Day parade, Stalin assumes to an unusual degree, as he has repeatedly done in the past, a warm, intimate, jovial mien.

Recently also Molotov has appeared in the juvenile literature as meeting groups of children—warm, interested in the children and their affairs and able to put everyone at his ease.

In the upbringing of children, corporal punishment is strictly forbidden and steadily inveighed against. "Parents must remember that nothing furthers more the growth of malignancy and stubbornness on the one hand, and on the other, of cowardliness, timidity, shyness . . . a spanking, however light, is no less insulting than a beating . . . measures of forcing are extreme measures which show that parents have been unable by other means to impose their authority on their children."[94] Everywhere the use of physical force against one's own, as distinct from the enemy, is presented as a sign of weakness. (An interesting side light on this objection by the Bolshevik to the need to use force is found in the violent controversies as to whether torture was used in the great trials. The violence of the denials can be related to the belief that such a use of torture would suggest that the Party was weaker than its own erring members, who are represented as strong but crushed beneath the weight of evidence of their own guilt. This, of course, does not apply to the use of any method against those who are regarded as being outside and therefore to be crushed by any means and totally annihilated.)

Instead of using force, the true leader should evoke, inspire, guide, and probe into the very souls of his followers. He himself must be full of initiative, he must work with the flame (s'ogon'kom), which should so animate him from within that it will glow so that all can see it. "Lenin did not rule long and his rule was like a bonfire. Some received light and warmth from it— others, fire and flame."

The bad leader is described as having limited his evaluation of people to their outward symptoms . . . contented himself with an evaluation of people according to their apparent behavior without looking into the motives of that behavior.[95] In contrast, the ideal leader of a collective farm is pictured as follows in an article in Pravda, January, 1949:[96]

> He sits in his spacious office. He is not a large man, but he is a well-built man. He is lively as mercury, he is cheerful and understands everything quickly, newspaper articles, scientific discoveries, songs and poetry. His head with its great protuberant brow and the small, regular features of a clean-shaven, round, clean Russian face is always somewhat inclined. He has a quick, soft Viatskii speech, with a manner of suddenly smiling and throwing his head back. There was united in him Bolshevik passion and muzhik calculatedness, bold directness and slyness, the capacity to organize masses and the capacity to look directly into the heart of an individual.

[94] L. Raskin, "Discipline and Culture in the Conduct of School Children," Young Guard, 1941.
[95] Discussion of Fadeyev's "Young Guard," in Molodoi Bol'shevik, June, 1947.
[96] G. Nikolaeva, "Features of the Future," Pravda, January 7, 1949.

Chapter 5

SOVIET OFFICIAL EXPECTATIONS REGARDING MOTIVATION

MOTIVATION FOR LEADERSHIP

We may now ask what are the official views on how the members of the leadership group are to be kept eternally on their toes, always straining toward higher goals, more culture, higher production, a fuller Soviet reality. There is, of course, an elaborate system of rewards, citations, decorations and orders, which, although they seem to an outsider to be enormously multiplied beyond the point of meaningfulness, nevertheless have definite positive value.

Bolshevik materialism admits of no idea of immortality such as is allowed for in most religious systems, but the promise of being enshrined in History probably fills the same function in giving a sense of self-continuation. A place on the Red Wall, after a funeral with Stalin as pallbearer, is possible for a highly placed Party member who dies in the odor of sanctity. This is sufficiently highly valued to provide the context for an informant to speculate about Dimitrov's death, whether he might not have consented to die when it would be most useful, since a place on the Red Wall was assured. Also, the sufferings and deprivations experienced by Party members in the exercise of their duty are believed to be alleviated by a full understanding of the part which they are playing in the Historical Process. A recent novel, *Unusual Summer*,[97] begins:

> Historical events are accompanied not only by a general excitement, "a rise or decay of the human spirit" but by extraordinary sufferings and privations which a man is unable to avert. For one who is conscious about these events, who understands that they constitute the course of history, or *who is himself one of the conscious motors,* these sufferings exist also. But such a man does not carry his sufferings as does one who is not thinking about the historical character of the events. [italics ours]

The Bolshevik ideal is one who is driven by his own internalized, deep involvement in the never-ending struggle, by his deep dissatisfaction with things as they are. This is one instance in which there has been a genuine and

---

[97] K. Fedin, "Unusual Summer" (*neobyknovennoye leto*), *Novyi Mir,* January, 1947, p. 37.

possibly successful attempt to build a revolution-derived pattern of behavior into the everyday life of the people in a society which no longer considers itself to be in a state of revolution. So the Bolshevik must see himself as living in a world in which "the merciless ideological fight of two systems, two world conceptions, two viewpoints regarding the future of mankind has always existed, still goes on and will be there permanently."[98]

In an article in *Bol'shevik*[99] for March, 1948, this struggle is spelled out:

> The principle of each development is the struggle between two contradictions, the struggle between the new and the old, between the dying and the born. The Marxist dialectic follows from the fact that the struggle between these two contradictions constitutes the internal content of the process of development. Stalin teaches: "Something is always dying in life. But what is dying is unwilling to die simply, but struggles for existence. Also something is being born, but it isn't born in a simple way, but whines, yells, insisting on its right to existence. The struggle between the old and the new, between what is dying and being born—is the basis of our development. This struggle is expressed in Soviet society in a totally new form, not through class struggles and cataclysms, but in the form of criticism and self criticism, the long range directing force of our development, a powerful instrument in the hands of the Party."

"The process of forming the new consciousness, the new morality, is very complicated. It is not a peaceful process, it is a difficult, tense struggle."[100]

This deep dissatisfaction, which is based on a recognition of the never-ending struggle, should be of such a character that each success, each new step forward should produce a desire to go even further. The young Bolshevik should learn to seek actively, eagerly, for that sense of having achieved, which, however, can never be repeated at the same level. To yield the same sense of satisfaction, the next achievement must be on a higher level.

This is stated explicitly as an educational goal. One should give to the little child, just learning to stand and walk, "tasks which he is up to but which are always more difficult, for example to walk independently an always greater distance from a definite place to a goal set beforehand,"[101] and, apart from training a child in specific qualities, parents must "awaken and support in each child the urge to do better than yesterday." At the same time, "it is important not to destroy but to strengthen his belief in himself, in his ability to become this better person, not to blunt but to sharpen in him the feeling of pride in that achievement which demands work, effort, self mastery, and emphasize

[98] K. Simonov, "Dramaturgy, Theatre and Life," *Literaturnaya Gazeta,* November 23, 1946.

[99] "Criticism and Self-Criticism, Principle of Development of Socialist Society," *Bol'shevik,* March 15, 1948.

[100] E. Bobovskaya and N. Chetunova, "Problems of the Family and Morality," *Oktyabr',* January, 1948.

[101] A. A. Liublinskaya, "On the Misdeeds of Children," *Family and School (Sem'ya i Shkola),* January, 1948.

always those large perspectives of social significance which are possible on the condition of such upward movement."[102] (It should be noted that, in the admonition to give the child something which he is capable of achieving and so to strengthen his belief in himself, the Soviet system is perpetuating what appears to be an important aspect of the pre-Soviet system of child rearing, in which each child was trained to be as strong as he could be rather than spurred on by competitive motives.)

The mechanics of this new Soviet conscience are stated in detail in an editorial, "Training in Purposefulness":[103]

> "Calm conscience" as a result of awareness of duty fulfilled gives man an immense joy. And the one who experiences "torments of conscience" from a bad action, a breach of social duty, feels terribly oppressed. . . . The habit of fulfilling that which one should do not only brings joy and satisfaction—calm consciousness as it is usually called—but develops a special sensitivity, that is, a special anxiety about whether all has been done and done properly.

We have at present no measure of how successful the Party has been in making this continuous, self-promoting anxiety a part of the personality of Party members or of future Party members. The demand for self-criticism —that is, the demand for criticism of Party members or of Komsomols by each other, coupled with a self-castigation, statements of error and promises of reform demanded from the one who is criticized—is a demand for the external conditions which would promote this continuous, productive anxiety. Simonov says:[104] "We have not only to go over what has been done badly but we should reproach ourselves for what we have not done sufficiently well from the standpoint of an artist of a socialist society."

In industry and agriculture we find the practice of confronting each individual, each work unit, with specific norms and then demanding that the norms be overfulfilled, so that mere fulfillment of a norm is automatically made unsatisfactory.

Throughout there is an ideal of combination of group pressure, actively exercised, and the response to group pressure of an individual whose conscience has been sensitized by lifelong admonition and training. If the individual's demand on himself, his continuous vigilant probing of his own behavior (Could he have done more? Should he have done more?) are developed to a degree equalling the group's public demands (made in the cell, at meetings, by local leaders of erring parents being brought to book, etc.), then a kind of balance between internal and external censure can be reached. The individual becomes wholly

---

[102] *Ibid.*

[103] "Training in Purposefulness," editorial in *Family and School* (*Sem'ya i Shkola*), March, 1948.

[104] K. Simonov, "Dramaturgy, Theatre and Life," *Literaturnaya Gazeta,* November 23, 1946.

repentant, is wholly absolved, and suddenly feels at one with the group. In the fictional materials from which the following illustrations are taken, one kind of pressure is emphasized more than the other. This is shown in a description of a collective farm meeting to expel a member who has systematically neglected her work and who is publicly rebuked by a feminine Hero of Socialist Labor:[105] "Citizen Kucherenko, are you not ashamed that the whole collective farm, the whole country, is working for you?"; and in the appeals of a father, reported approvingly in the educational literature, in which he says to his 14-year old daughter:[106]

> You are already fourteen; soon you will be grown-up. But if now you do not want to help your brother, how will you work in the collective, help comrades, lend support to those behind schedule? Remember, you will have a bad time in life. An egoist is not liked in any work collective. And your work will give you no satisfaction or joy if you will hold yourself aloof and think only about yourself!

In a postwar novel,[107] a husband who was a deserter, whose wife rejects him for his desertion, gives himself up in order to be allowed to enter a penal battalion to wash away the blemish from his life. When at the end of the war he returns, after having fought courageously, his wife still will not accept him nor will his former friends and neighbors. And the former deserter says to his wife:

> You know, before I had thought the most dreadful thing was to undergo the punishment of the government. But what happened was that Life punished much more strongly, through you, the children, the collective.

The reliance on well-inculcated internal standards is expressed in such statements as the following:[108]

> In the factory, in the plant, the *peredovoi* (advance guard) young person is that young man or young girl who works honestly, according to shock methods, who carries out and surpasses the standards, who fights for the high quality of the production, who treats the lathe, the machines and the tools carefully, who masters the techniques of work and increases his own qualifications.

This statement, which stresses an entirely internal motivation which should theoretically operate in the absence of supervision or group pressures, will be balanced by such a statement as the following:[109]

---

[105] A. Agronovsky, "Day of Labor" (*Trudyen'*), *Literaturnaya Gazeta,* July 21, 1948, p. 2.

[106] I. A. Pechernikova, *Teaching the Schoolboy to Share in the Family Work,* Uchpedgiz, 1948.

[107] Y. Mal'tsev, "From the Whole of the Heart," *Oktyabr',* Issue 10, 1948, p. 86.

[108] Tenth Congress of the All-Union Leninist Communist League of Youth, April 11–21, 1936 (*X s'ezd Vsesoyuznovo Leninskovo Kommunisticheskovo Soiuza Molodezhi 11–21 aprelia 1936 g.*), stenographic account.

[109] A. A. Liublinskaya, "On the Misdeeds of Children," *Family and School* (*Sem'ya i Shkola*), January, 1948.

The older children become, the more important for their moral countenance and therefore for their behavior becomes the Collective of their comrades, its attitudes, its evaluations. Rules of conduct adopted by the Collective become binding for the one who feels himself a member of this Collective; the evaluation by the Collective of various traits of character becomes absolute for each of its members.

I shall quote at some length one fictional account of the way in which individual sinfulness, as defined by the Soviets, is acted upon by the collective of the Komsomol group so as to bring the individual back into the type of accord with the group which is usually associated with religious absolution and which actually, in this modern Soviet account, uses conventional religious terminology. This account is taken from the story of a group of apprentices, one of whom, Aleha, has had his character distorted into individualism by his remaining to care for his mother in an area occupied by the Germans. In the foundry where he goes to work, he attempts to do too much by himself and sends his partner away to show that he can manage a furnace without assistance. An explosion occurs. In the subsequent investigation he also lies. Here follows a condensed account of the Komsomol meeting:[110]

(The day comes when Aleha applies to join the Komsomol. He goes through many painful apprehensive moments as he asks the old master (ironmaker) to recommend him and confesses to his *Komsorg* (Komsomol organizer) that he lied.) But at the meeting Aleha again understood that not so easily and quickly could all his sins be forgotten. Having finished recounting his autobiography, Aleha fell silent, awaiting the further moves of the meeting. Igor B. took the floor. "Our bureau has decided to accept the comrade. But this does not yet mean anything. The main thing is you, fellows, the Komsomol mass. We await your decision. To accept the comrade or to abstain. Let us think. . . ." Aleha listened to these words with terror. They resounded in his very heart. Igor continued: "Comrade Polovodov (Aleha) has placed himself beyond the collective. He wanted alone to make use of the success and joy of Komsomol work. And it is unknown, had everything gone smoothly, how far he would have risen in his pride. Let him today answer all of us what he now thinks about himself, about us, about the Komsomol, about life. This moment is such that a man's soul can be seen even without glasses. So, say everything that you think, Polovodov." . . . Many noticed that Aleha was trembling. His agitation immediately transmitted itself to all the others sitting in the hall, quickly from one to another, as a wave in the sea is stirred by wind. Everyone felt simultaneous pain and joy. Pain, because they clearly saw a man suffering and understood precisely from what (he was suffering) and already wished that he might no longer suffer. And joy because he was with them and was not separated, withdrawn any more. This could be seen by his sparkling eyes, his quivering lips which were preparing themselves already to pronounce other words, finally by his hands, stretched out uncertainly, with the fingers spread apart, as if he wanted to encompass in one embrace all those sitting there in the hall. . . . No one was indifferent any

---

[110] V. Kurochkin, "Brigade of the Smart" (*Brigada smyshlenykh*), *Oktyabr'*, September, 1947.

longer. The soul (of each) wished to express itself. But the rules of the meeting were rigid, the chairman sat severe, immovable. He gave the floor to no one except Aleha. The boys wished that Aleha would take courage. He was now their comrade. They recognized this. After such a sudden frank expression of mutual feeling, Aleha did not really have to continue. Everyone understood what further he wanted to say. But Aleha himself unexpectedly calmed down and firmly decided to express his intentions to the meeting. "I, fellows, am not going to lie to you. What is there, is there. I am here in front of you as at confession. I cannot feel my hands and feet, I feel so good. Do you still think that I like it better alone than with you? It is not so. Alone, I suffer, that is all. I am not glad to be by myself. But now it will be a completely different matter. Now I'll begin to work even better. . . . Forgive me if I said anything to affront you." On this his speech ended and the meeting prepared to vote. Aleha felt that he was experiencing in himself some yet incomprehensible grace which affected all his feelings, urges, wishes. He had never imagined that it could be so pleasant. It was as if all were changing in him, each little vein becoming stronger.

The preparation for such a scene is allowed for in such pedagogical instructions as these:[111]

> Give him time to think and torment himself over the solution, but in the end, if necessary, point out to the adolescent that there is but one way, that of duty (in this case, to confess before his teacher and schoolmates).

The likenesses and differences between the old type of Russian motivation and the new Soviet type are brought out very strikingly in these examples. Under the old system, a child was reared and admonished by a very large number of persons of different castes and was given different sets of standards, which were very loosely tied together by the teachings of the Orthodox Church and were reinforced, in the teachings of peasants and nurses, by a large number of miscellaneous supernatural fears. Fear of being cut off from one's own group, fear of supernatural punishments, confusion among the many standards of conduct which were illustrated and enjoined, a diffuse sense of guilt which was willing to take upon itself a variety of sins committed perhaps only in thought, these characterized this earlier type of character. During the development of the early intelligentsia, with their rigorous revolutionary ideals, there seems to have been some narrowing of these multiple authority figures in the life of the child and the emergence of the demand, which we now characterize as Bolshevik, for a more rigidly defined, focused, and unyielding character in which forgiveness played much less of a role and a man judged both himself and his fellows more harshly. At the same time, theories of what community and collective life meant, the substitution of the social group for a supernatural, priest-mediated authority seemed, in the early days of the Soviet Union, to be placing all the emphasis outside the individual and encouraging a type of edu-

---

[111] "Training in a Sense of Duty," editorial, *Family and School* (*Sem'ya i Shkola*), June, 1948.

cation in which the feeling of shame, if one were discovered and rebuked, was the behavior type which was most likely to result. This was particularly so during the period in which the family was regarded as unimportant, and the group alone, whether it was in kindergarten, of Komsomols, or of fellow workers, was supposed to hear confessions and to administer public rebukes.

Today the literature suggests that the Soviet Union is moving toward a type of education which resembles (but, as we shall see, also differs from) the older Russian form of many authority figures operating upon an individual sense of general guilt and unworthiness. The authority of the parents has been re-emphasized after the attempts to reduce it during the first fifteen years of the regime, and parents are now recognized as the principal figures in the early life of the child, which means the reintroduction of persons of greater age and status as authority figures, and this is conducive to the formation of internalized standards of conduct. Furthermore, parents are seen as only one part of a completely harmonized attempt to bring up the young in the way they should go. "What does it mean," asks Likhacheva,[112] "to bring up a fighter for communism? It means that the school and the family and the society must bring up the young man." This bringing to bear of all available forces upon the target is a familiar Bolshevik theory of tactics, here applied to education. Instead of the old inconsistencies between standards and sanctions presented by many individuals in the environment, one set of standards is to be presented. When the parents fail, the Komsomol steps in, or the school may even apply to a trade-union to persuade an erring father to take an interest in his son's report card. "Aiding the strengthening of family relations and ties, socialist society thereby makes fast in the people many of those high qualities which characterize the moral countenance of the Soviet citizen."[113] And, in comparing the old and the new, a Soviet student of education puts his finger on the greater concentration on a unified effort today:[114]

> Belinsky wrote (about the pre-revolutionary school) that the family must make a man out of the child; the school, an educated citizen ready to struggle for the best ideals. . . . Now the school and the family are joined in one wish: to nurture in us the traits of a real Soviet man, make us educated persons devoted to our people, to our mother country.

Each of the agencies which impinge on the child are to put all their effort, all their thought into doing the same thing. This should produce a type of motivation and will power which does not occur in Western democracies, where there are a variety of different courses presented to a child in whom, ideally, the will to choose among them has been cultivated. Nor was such a character

---

[112] N. Likhacheva, "Mother-Tutoress," *Family and School* (*Sem'ya i Shkola*), March, 1948.

[113] G. M. Sverdlov, *Marriage and Family* (*Brak i sem'ya*) (pamphlet), Uchpedgiz, 1946.

[114] *Stories by Graduates of Moscow Schools,* Detgiz, 1947, p. 8.

structure cultivated in pre-Soviet Russia. Instead, educational experiences tended to develop a diffuse sense of guilt and of responsibility, not for acts of will, but for the merest thought or intention.

Under this new Soviet character structure, the will should be developed without, however, any sense of the possibility of choice. If the child looks into itself, it should find only the same standards as those expressed all around it and which, when his parent errs, he is—in Soviet fiction—also ready to express. All authority figures converge upon him, and he, like Aleha, is to feel completely at one with and submissive to this standard, which is both inside him and outside him. "Soviet man feels himself an indivisible part of the industrial or social collective to which he is bound, with which he labors. Soviet man experiences achievements or lack of them in communal matters as his own personal successes or failures. He feels his moral responsibility for communal matters and thus he develops a sense of duty."[115] "The personal interests of Soviet man must combine harmoniously with communal interests; the personal must always be subordinated to the social."

It must be recognized that in such an ideal there should be no need for force, for physical coercion. The conception of character is one in which the individual, himself, is able to receive grace from a group whose standards he shares and so, with the past forgotten—the secular Soviet version of forgiveness —go on to a higher moral level. We shall see in later sections how incompatible this ideal, which would need no reinforcement by coercion or by political police, is with the Soviet demand for total control over every detail of the life of children. A character structure such as that described here is congruent with a complete respect for all human beings in a society, with a lack of hierarchy, and with a lack of any sense of gulf between a group ruling and a group ruled. But the leadership of the Soviet Union seems to have inherited and developed, from sources of its own, a deep contempt for the mass of the people and an attitude toward children, as individuals to be subordinated and ignored until they attain years of discretion, which do not provide the necessary conditions for the development of the kind of ideal character structure described here.

Nevertheless, the political implications of the ideal character (which is always spurred on to new achievement because each achievement serves to define the necessary next step) are worth considering, especially in the choice of propaganda themes. Any propaganda which suggests present failure to the Soviet Union may merely provoke angry denial, but it may also act as a spur to greater activity. This type of personality is essentially puritanical, feeding upon a sense of its own deficiencies while presenting to the outer world a façade of smugness and self-satisfaction. To the extent that the Soviet Union has succeeded in pro-

---

[115] "Training in a Sense of Duty," editorial, *Family and School* (*Sem'ya i Shkola*), June, 1948.

ducing such a personality in its leadership group, it will have to be reckoned with.

We shall turn presently to the way in which these ideals of behavior are modified by the practical need to run a state, to produce manufactured goods, to equip an army, to produce food for a vast population, etc., and to what extent the actual administration of the Soviet Union has taken its models not from this Bolshevik theory of leadership by a self-propelled, self-critical, completely dedicated group, but from the traditional methods of control of the Tsarist state supplemented by observation of other modern autocratically organized nations.

EXPECTATIONS CONCERNING THE MASSES AND CHILDREN

We may now set this picture of the ideal leadership pattern, the type of character, and relationship to the led against the picture of what the led, the masses and the children, are expected to contribute to the whole. We have seen in the earlier discussion of relationships between different levels that each person who is in any sort of leadership role is expected to partake, in his relationship to those below him, of some of the behavior of the top leader upon whom he models his conduct. The Komsomol is to be in the vanguard everywhere—in industry, in society, in the family—giving the smallest and the greatest task his full attention. The parent, any parent, is seen as totally responsible for his or her children as is the Party secretary for the cell, the chairman for the collective.

Much of the literature suggests a single line from leader to smallest child, with those on the lowest levels of age or skill or knowledge of Bolshevism looking up, aspiring toward higher levels from which they in turn will serve as models for those below them. But this picture is confused by another in which the Party is a distillate from the whole group, fed by children, by youth, by workers and farmers, but is essentially a narrow group to which most of the population neither aspires nor is expected to aspire. The view of both children and masses is quite different, depending on whether they are all seen as future Party members (when they have advanced enough in wisdom or stature), or whether they are seen as a great mass from which only a very few, with the appropriate spiritual ambition and moral strength, are to be drawn. When the non-Party masses are viewed as many who will never join the Party, not even in the persons of their unborn grandchildren, they present considerable confusion and difficulty to Bolshevik theories of authority. We have, in the works of Lenin and in the early congresses, discussions about the relationship between Party and non-Party: "In order to realize the leadership of the Party it is indispensable that the Party be encompassed by hundreds of non-Party mass *apparati* (staff) which constitute tentacles in the hands of the Party with the aid of which it transmits its will to the working class, and the working class from [being] dispersed masses, becomes the army of the Party."[116]

The dictatorship (of the proletariat) cannot be achieved without some transmission belts from the vanguard of the masses to the leading class and from it to the mass of the laboring class. "The dictatorship of the proletariat consists in the leading directives of the Party plus the carrying out of these directives by the mass organizations of the proletariat, plus the transformation of the life of the population."[117]

With the lack of clarity regarding the relationship of the Party to the masses goes a fear that some other center will develop which will compete for their allegiance, sometimes localized outside the Soviet Union, using propaganda, and sometimes inside, existing as remnants of the bourgeois past. Sometimes it is feared that different elements within the Party as well as among the non-Party masses may be won over to some counterrevolutionary position. Stalin, at the time of the 15th Congress, 1927,[118] described these indifferent elements as *boloto*, a swamp, a word borrowed from the terminology of the French Constituante which described the undecided and wavering middle which was dominated in turn by the different extremes. Said Stalin, "Discussion is an appeal to the swamp. The Opposition appeals to it in order to tear off a portion. And they actually tear off the worse part. The Party appeals to it to tear off the better part and to attract it to active Party life. As a result the swamp has to *determine for itself what it will do,* despite all its inertness. As a result of all of these appeals it actually does make this determination, one part going to the opposition and one part going to the Party, thereby it ceases to exist as swamp." [italics ours] Here the Party is seen as contending, against strong counterforces, for those over whom there should be no contention. In 1928, Stalin, quoting Lenin, said:[119] "*petit bourgeois* elements surround the proletariat from every side with a *petit bourgeois* atmosphere which permeates it and acts as a corrupting influence on the proletariat, debases it, makes it lose morality." [italics ours] This fear of the corruption which may spring up in that which is lifeless and inert has not diminished with the disappearance of those *petit bourgeois* elements who were once identified as a source of danger. The Bolsheviks seem to have difficulty in believing that the enemy is ever completely destroyed: "We have defeated the enemies of the Party, the opportunists of all shades, national deviations of all types but the remnants of their ideologies are still living in the heads of indi-

---

[116] Lenin and Stalin, *Partiinoye stroitel'stvo,* Vol. 2, pp. 322–23.

[117] Lenin, *Polnoye sobraniye,* Vol. 25, p. 96.

[118] J. Stalin, in a Report of the 15th All-Union Congress of the Communist Party (B) (*XV s'ezd Vsesoyuznoi Kommunisticheskoi Partii (B)*), stenographic account, Moscow, 1928, p. 173.

[119] J. Stalin, "Of the Right Danger in the CPSU," addressed to the Plenum of Moscow Committee and Moscow Control Commission of CPSU, October, 1928.

vidual members of the Party and make themselves heard," said Stalin, in 1934.[120]

This danger is now more explicitly attributed to forces outside the Soviet Union, but this does not change the essential attitudes of the leadership toward the dangers lurking in the undifferentiated swamp. In a 1947 postwar story,[121] a youth is described who

> kept apart from the collective. He feared his personal success would be stolen. It is because there still operates in him as with some other peasant adolescents a yeast (*zakvaska*) foreign to us. . . . Capitalists still today are attempting to build their final defense line in the hearts of men. They would be *glad to tear away from us* those who are weak, impatient; who believe little in the future, who, finally, have not yet learned to believe. Would not the enemy indeed wish that the little heart of a peasant adolescent should become the bastion of their ideals?" [italics ours]

This theme is reiterated in the recent attacks on the West and on influences brought back to the Soviet Union by those returning from the West. "There still exist people who, after the victory, brought us the most thin and light fluids, alien to our psychology. The fluids have to be examined, named and perhaps through this, rendered harmless. The admiration of bourgeois culture is one of those fluids. It seems to be innocent in itself, . . . The delicate scent of repose comes from these little things—these bits of foreign ideas—a cadaverous odor of prosperity."[122] From 1928 to 1949 the essential theme has not changed, the fear that there is an indifferent, apathetic mass of people who are dangerous because responsive to alien influences, whose indifference can be activated—unless they are completely protected—into a lethal corruption of the whole society. That which is almost dead may live again—in the wrong way.

This ambiguous attitude toward the undifferentiated masses whose relationship to the Party is so badly defined is complicated by the theory of purges. Yaroslavski[123] said:

> That is why we have to expel from the Party from time to time not only people originating from non-proletarian classes who are more susceptible to disintegration than proletarians, but also proletarians who have fallen under the petty bourgeois elemental forces of the past.

There is also the insistence upon keeping the Party itself clean and strong by constantly purging its ranks. As a 1933 directive stated: "The purging will raise to a high degree the feeling entertained by every Party member of responsibility for his organization."[124] But what happens to those who are purged?

[120] J. Stalin, Report of 17th Congress of CPSU, 1934.
[121] Kurochkin, *op. cit.*
[122] P. Antokol'skii, "About Poetry, Education of the Youth and Culture," *Znamya*, January, 1947.
[123] E. Yaroslavski, *Verification and Purging of the Party Ranks*, Moscow, 1933, p. 11.
[124] Directive of January, 1933, Plenum of Central Control Commission of CPSU.

Unless they are physically liquidated, which was only true for larger numbers in the late thirties, they remain in the population, either to be actively rehabilitated and reinstated or to contribute significantly to the dangerous, unreliable quality of the swamp, the wavering, undecided mass of the people. This is a view of the population which is apt to support a belief in the necessity for rigid authoritarian controls rather than for education in moral autonomy, and it is reflected in the attempts to protect the Soviet population against foreign propaganda of all sorts, in admonitions to parents to watch carefully the companions with whom their children associate and by whom they can be corrupted. A belief that the children of one's neighbors, for whom under another part of Soviet theory one is also responsible, are sources of corruption obviously tends to breed suspicion and a desire for more rigid control.

A second attitude toward the masses, and to some extent toward children, is a reliance upon them to provide the energy through which the Party is able to carry out its will. The masses of today provide the present energy; the children, "the Soviet citizens of tomorrow who are the children of today," provide the future sources of energy. Taking this view of the masses, Stalin said, in 1937:[125] "Like Antaeus, the Bolsheviks are strong in that they maintain their contact with their mother, the masses, which gave them birth, fed them and brought them up." On the other hand, Maksimovskii could say, at the 10th Party Congress in 1921, that the Party should "put ourselves in the position of a pedagogue, not a nurse,"[126] and Stalin,[127] "The distinction between the vanguard of the proletariat and the main body of the working class, between Party members and non-Party members will continue so long as classes exist, so long as the proletariat continues replenishing its ranks with newcomers from other classes, as long as the working class as a whole is deprived of the opportunity of raising itself to the level of the vanguard. But the Party would cease to be a Party if this distinction were widened into a rupture; if it were to isolate itself and break from the non-Party masses." This was said in 1928, and in an article in May, 1949, in Bol'shevik,[128] it is said: "the consciousness of their nearness with the people, the skill in leading the masses, define the main features of an active purposeful Bolshevik." In Komsomol'skaia Pravda, in 1949, an editorial insists: "Any Komsomol organization will wither, will perish, if it breaks this most important Party principle and separates itself from the young." This location of the source of energy in the masses appears in the impassioned speech

---

[125] J. Stalin, Mastering Bolshevism, Report to the 1937 Plenum of the Central Committee of the CPSU, printed in Bol'shevik, April 1, 1937.

[126] Maksimovskii, 10th Congress of the Russian Communist Party (B) (X s'ezd Rossiiskoi Kommunisticheskoi Partii (B)), stenographic account, Moscow, 1928.

[127] J. Stalin, "Foundations of Leninism" (Osnovi Leninizma) as in Stalin, Leninism, New York, 1928.

[128] N. Ozerov, "The Image of the Bolshevik," Bol'shevik, May, 1949.

of the chairman of a collective farm, reported in *Pravda*.[129] The chairman has been listening to the comments of the man in charge of accounts, who claims that there is no "secret" for the success of the collective except accuracy, consistency, and high agricultural technique.

> "It's not true" interrupted Pyotr Alekseyevich (the chairman). . . . "We have a secret. Our secret is something that many chairmen underestimate and which our Party always puts at the head of everything. It's ideological education of the people." His words sounded strong and passionate. "The organization of labor, agricultural technique, connections with science, all these are very important matters, but at the first difficulty they become empty ciphers if there is no Party soul in the collective farm . . . ideological education for us is just like wings for an airplane."

This "Party soul," this source of energy which lies in the people and is to be used to bring success to Party enterprises, was dramatized in the Soviet film *The Peasants*, in which the Party secretary, faced with a recalcitrant, rebellious collective farm committee who wished to distribute all the collectively grown pigs, called on the spontaneous devotion of the mass of the collective farm members to stage a demonstration of extra, voluntary work and turned the tide at the meeting.

The masses are thus seen as a source of strength and energy, and just as the leaders are credited with special foresight, so the masses are credited with a kind of insight.

Stalin expressed formal adherence to this point of view in 1937:[130]

> We leaders see things, events and people from one side only, I would say from above. Our field of vision, consequently, is more or less limited. The masses, on the contrary, see things, events, and people from another side, I would say, from below. Their field of vision, consequently, is also, in a certain degree, limited. To receive a correct solution to the question, these two experiences must be united (*obedinit*). Only in such a case will the leadership be correct.

Where the leader is to be, above all things, controlled, reserved, unimpassioned, the people are to have a "passionate Bolshevik desire" (*strastnoye zhelaniye*); "if a thing is passionately desired, everything can be achieved, everything can be overcome." In "Lamp of Il'ich" the electrification of collective farms is promised for the whole country, and the question is asked: "But where to find such a force capable of accomplishing such a difficult undertaking?"[131] The authors of the electrification plan answer: "We have such a force. The force is the people. If the people wish, nothing is impossible for them." And as soon as

---

[129] G. Nikolaeva, "Features of Future," *Pravda*, January 7–8, 1949.

[130] J. Stalin, *Mastering Bolshevism*, Report to the 1937 Plenum of the Central Committee of the CPSU, printed in *Bol'shevik*, April 1, 1937.

[131] E. Kriger, "Lamp of Il'ich," *Friendly Youngsters* (*Druzhnyie Rebyata*), December, 1947.

the plan was born, people in far-off and deaf villages began to compose a song about light, "Wires are humming, laughing, electricity now burns. All victories are possible, if the Party orders so."

This statement is an example of the combination of two omnipotence fantasies, the old Social Revolutionary fantasy of the overpowering energy of the masses combined with the Bolshevik fantasy of omnipotence by conscious control. This same zestful energy which is attributed to the people is also attributed to youth. A young Komsomol girl is represented as saying:[132] "I want to be a mechanic and I believe that I shall become one. . . . Indeed, for us, for Soviet youth, the situation is this. What one plans one can achieve, if only one has the desire, the persistence, and the will."

In the educational system there is great emphasis upon developing these desirable mass qualities of strength and endurance, of zest and enthusiasm in the citizen of tomorrow. So the official pedagogy[133] insists: "Precisely in the first days of an infant's existence, training in this importance quality (endurance) should begin; naturally at this age one can talk only of training in physical endurance."

From the earliest days of the Soviet Union there has been an emphasis on physical care of children and an expressed interest in the child as a future citizen, necessary to society, who should "enter life properly prepared, communistically reared, and strong muscled."[134]

Throughout the educational system, a double emphasis is seen which can be taken as a reflection, in much more open form, of the attitude which the leadership group holds toward the masses. Throughout the discussion of child care and training, although there is frequent reference to the importance of maintaining a child's self-confidence, zest, and sensitivity, there is also great emphasis upon control, upon the establishment of habits of obedience, punctuality, neatness, thrift. Children must be firmly accustomed to "daily, regular, perhaps small but sensible efforts without waiting for an occasion for some heroic deed."[135] This admonition can be contrasted with the Komsomol statement that "the entire pathos of the Komsomol work must be carried into studying."[136] The Komsomols are bade: "take possession of the entire treasure house of human knowledge and culture."[137] For pupils whose wills are to be educated, "it is not enough to inspire them with great aims and ideals. . . . The best training is in the accurate scrupulous fulfillment of daily modest ordinary

[132] Komsomol'skaia Pravda, March 31, 1949, p. 4.

[133] "Training in Endurance," Family and School (Sem'ya i Shkola), January, 1948.

[134] Perel and Lyubimova, The Legal Position of the Child in the Family (Pravovoy polozheniye rebyonka u sem'ya), Uchpedgiz, 1932.

[135] Extract from Chap. 14, Pedagogy, Moscow, 1948, pp. 315–17.

[136] Tenth Congress of the All-Union Leninist Communist League of Youth, April 11–21, 1936.

[137] P. Razmyslov, "A. S. Makarenko's Views on Family Upbringing," Family and School (Sem'ya i Shkola), March, 1948.

duties."[138] "Children must know exactly their bedtime, time of play and preparation of lessons. . . . Children must have a capacity to repress, to control themselves." "Sexual education must consist in the development of that intimate respect for sexual questions which is called chastity. An ability to control one's feelings, imagination, rising desires, is an important ability." Girls who successfully subordinate their romantic interests to the demands of group activities are glorified in the model-setting literature.

The familiar emphasis upon the crucial importance of the smallest possible detail reappears here also. "Each action, each conversation, each word, either helps the blossoming of a child's spiritual forces, or on the contrary breaks and maims his spirit, accustoming him to rudeness, lying, and other bad qualities in upbringing, in this many-sided, deep process of personality formation, there is nothing that may be considered a trifle."[139] And with this importance of every trifle goes a demand for the continuance of parental responsibility which is hardly compatible with the development of independence and individual will. "The older a child becomes the more heightened becomes the parents' responsibility for his upbringing as well as for their own behavior."[140]

Another dichotomy is found in the attitude toward the imagination of children, which, again, may be regarded as a clue to the attitudes toward spontaneous inventiveness in the masses. On the one hand, Soviet pedagogy insists on the importance of play: "Our children must know how to dream and to realize their dreams in reality. . . . The development of fantasy is an important task of the educator. For example, children prepare to fly to the moon. They represent in play that which has not taken place in reality. But such play arose as a result of stories of the remarkable flights accomplished by our fliers. These stories have created the conviction in our children that the heroes will accomplish ever new exploits, that they will continue the conquest of cosmic space. . . . Obviously such make-believe is to be permitted and encouraged by the educator."[141] But, on the other hand: "The educator does not permit inventions which may create in children incorrect representations, incorrect attitudes to life. If children represent Soviet soldiers, fliers, workers, it is very important that their actions and words correspond to the role they adopt." In the recent critical survey of a nineteenth-century writer, Schneerman[142] distinguishes between two kinds of imagination (*mechta*), the creative imagination and the narcotic imagination, and adds: "The ability of the young Soviet generation to guide their

[138] A. S. Makarenko, *Book for Parents* (*Kniga dlya roditelei*), Gospolitizdat, 1937.

[139] N. Y. Yudina, "Parental Authority," *Family and School* (*Sem'ya i Shkola*), April, May, 1946.

[140] *Ibid.*

[141] D. Mendzherritskii, "Children's Play," *Play of Children*, Uchpedgiz, 1948. (Collection of articles from the magazine *Pre-School Education*.)

[142] A. L. Shneerman, "Problems of the Psychology of Upbringing in the Course of General Pedagogy," *Soviet Pedagogy* (*Sovetskaya Pedagogika*), Vol. 4, 1949, p. 61.

imagination, to develop it in the necessary direction, to utilize creative force in the interest of the communistic transformation of our Motherland—those are the concrete problems of the psychology of upbringing." And "In the process of play, parents should give the child as much freedom of action as possible, but only as long as the play proceeds properly."[143]

In this insistence on an imagination which can fly to the moon but must still be so rigidly channeled that no mistake is made in the play-acting of the role of a Soviet fireman, we find the familiar Bolshevik conviction of being able to harness all the forces in nature and in human nature and to use them for their own purposes. It is more difficult to get material which demonstrates attitudes toward the masses and the need for controlling them. This material, while it may be phrased in a manner protective and educational for children, contains contempt that denotes a lower level of expectation for adults. In official literature the masses must be spoken of with respect, but informal evidence suggests this same attitude of exercising rigid control and at the same time wishing to call forth the maximum zest obtainable.

The demand for zest is open and continuous. "All work in the representations of Soviet children is joyful work. . . ."[144]

> The clarity of the perspectives of our magnificent future, unshakable confidence in the triumph of Communism, awareness of moral superiority over those hostile to Communism, give rise to those feelings of cheerfulness and joy-in-life, which are imprescriptible traits of Soviet people. . . . Communistic ideas are the most life-asserting, most light and bright, most optimistic ideas of mankind, a counterbalance to all ideas of "world sorrow," man-hatred, slavery and oppression.

"Of course, in the workaday life of the family unavoidable difficulties occur, deprivations and losses which bring sadness and cause suffering. Only real courage allows one to bear up steadfastly and to reestablish soon the temporarily disturbed, basically cheerful and joyful tone of family life."[145] Optimism and cheerfulness are seen as essential traits of Soviet people. Children should be prevented from ever feeling lonely, and all exclusive concentration on their own feelings, all withdrawal and misanthropy should be actively watched for. Critics excoriate novelists whose work is permeated with "a feeling of tiredness," who use "weak and anesthetic words," or who permit their characters pages of "weeping, sobbing, groaning." Feelings of "contemplation and passivity" are equally disapproved of.

These expressed fears of what may happen if children are left alone, if workers are not continuously subjected to inspiration and pressure, if people

---

[143] A. S. Makarenko, "Lectures on the Upbringing of Children," *Book for Parents* (*Kniga dlya roditelei*), 1937.

[144] "Influence of an Educator on Content of Children's Play," *Pre-School Education* (*Doshkol'noe Vospitanie*), August, 1948.

[145] "On Cheerfulness and *Joie-de-vivre*," *Family and School* (*Sem'ya i Shkola*), May, 1948.

are allowed to read about characters who are melancholy and introspective provide information not about the children, workers, or readers, but about the members of the regime who, through their exhortations to joyousness and optimism and their attempts to control those they exhort, indicate apprehension that the fear and depression which has been officially outlawed will break through in others and in their own highly controlled personalities.

While it is loudly proclaimed that "we will permit no one to poison our youth with the venom of disbelief, pessimism and decadence,"[146] the tale is told of the aviator who almost lost his life because of an intrusive feeling of pity,[147] of the boy who pretends to be tubercular in order to stay with his mother, in whom something "did not grow together inside."[148] It is officially stated that "the socialistic regime liquidated the tragedy of loneliness from which men of the capitalist world suffer,"[149] but the juvenile literature is filled with lonely children and with incomplete families, and it is probably significant that the critics—following the official line—are able to find so many instances of characters in plays who are "lonely, injured, suffering from disassociation of personality." One postwar novel[150] describes vividly the feeling of Soviet men sent abroad after the war: "the idea that we might remain alone at the foot of this indifferent cliff, somewhere between Europe and Asia, among all those castanets, black-eyed Spanish girls, placid policemen with knuckle-dusters in their pockets; this idea that we might be left without mercy in a place where we were not necessary to anybody (and we for our part felt: 'why the devil do we need all that?')—this very idea made us shudder."

A recent novel[151] covertly satirized vividly the fear which lies behind the whole Bolshevik attitude in the character of the Communist Izvekov, who in the novel is represented as being completely indifferent to the regret which the writer, Pastukhov, expresses, that in pursuit of such noble aims as those of the Revolution, "in the struggle for good, man is obliged to do so much that is evil." During an offensive of the Red army, the military unit to which Izvekov is attached is allowed to hunt a wolf in the forest. Someone succeeds in hitting the wolf, and Izvekov suspects that it is he himself who has done so. Suddenly he sees the wounded wolf not far from where he is and fires a second shot. After the wolf is dead, Izvekov analyzes his reason for firing that unnecessary second shot. Suddenly he realizes that, beyond all reason, he was pushed by unconscious fear of the mortally wounded and no longer dangerous beast. In the same

[146] *Komsomol'skaia Pravda,* March 31, 1949, p. 2.

[147] R. Fraerman, *Far Voyage (Dal'neye plavaniye),* 1946.

[148] Kurochkin, *op. cit.*

[149] Editorial, "Education in Comradeship and Friendship," *Family and School (Sem'ya i Shkola),* April, 1948.

[150] L. Kasil, and S. Mikhalkov, "Europe At Left," *Zvezda,* September, 1946.

[151] K. Fedin, "Unusual Summer," *Novyi Mir,* 1945 (4,5,6,7,8,9); 1947 (1,5,9,12); 1948 (4,10).

instant that he confessed this fear to himself, he became ashamed and felt that all his body was bathed in a hot sweat.

This political fable may be analyzed at several levels: as a satire on the Bolshevik who is supposed (a) never to feel fear; (b) who is supposed, if he feels fear, never to express it; and (c) who is supposed to have such foresight and judgment that he would not commit such an unnecessary act as shooting an animal which was not dangerous. At a deeper level, this fable also expresses the Bolshevik belief that the least fear may lead to panic, to a completely false judgment of the potential dangerousness of the enemy. Such an animal might then appear able to destroy first oneself and then a whole village. Against such avalanche fears, very rigid defenses are necessary.

In summary, we find that Bolshevik ideas of leadership and the character appropriate to leadership provide for an alert, all-responsible, never-satisfied conscience, constantly stimulated by one achievement to attempt a higher one, which ideas are complemented by a picture of those who are led that is confused as to whether they are to be seen as future leaders, future members of the Party, or as permanent members of a mass and subject to appeals which may lure them away from the Party. These ideas are complicated further by the need for rigid control and continuous watchfulness enjoined upon the leadership, which makes them, while officially relying upon the strength, enthusiasm, and energy provided by the masses, fearful that unless the most rigid, minute, continuous, protective, and directive control is maintained, catastrophe will result.

Chapter 6

THE PLACE OF THE POLITICAL POLICE
IN THE SOVIET AUTHORITY SYSTEM

We have now traced in some detail the Soviet ideal of the relationship between the Party and the masses and between the leader and the people and also the way in which the leadership group is supposed both to draw upon the energy and strength of the people and yet to remain above the people, guiding and directing them because of a closer contact with the Truth. We have discussed some of the discrepancies within this ideal; for example, the way in which members of each leadership level are expected to be models for those beneath them, while those beneath them, although owing them legal allegiance as officials of superior rank who speak in the name of the Party, owe them no personal allegiance, but instead are expected to give their personal devotion to the top leadership of the Party only. Motivation is expected to result from such a close awareness of the never-ending struggle in the world and from such an urge to reach ever higher levels of achievement that each new activity must, to be equally satisfying, be better than the last. The people themselves, the masses and the children, are supposed to contribute a spontaneous energy which nevertheless must always be manipulated, directed, and kept within bounds. Every area of life is brought within the political, and the whole of each individual's personality is conceived as being involved in anything which he does.

This whole theory is conspicuously lacking in any theory of organization, and Lenin could, as late as 1917–18, define the ideal society as one in which there would be no differentiation in function, no difference between leaders and led, no officialdom, and no hierarchy, when the state should have "withered away." Meanwhile there was an enormous chaotic society, ravaged by war and revolution, which had to be not only reconstructed, but also transformed economically and politically. The Bolshevik leadership, while advancing the ideal of a society in which the conscience of each fully devoted citizen would be the only necessary control over his behavior, was committed to a view of absolute Truth which made it impatient of any delay in the realization of the ideal. Finally, the leadership came from a society in which bureaucratic controls had always been strong, and, while they had rebelled against Tsarist controls, they had nevertheless had little actual experience of any other way of administering a national state.

Within this varied set of conditions and amid the impatience and fear which seem to accompany dictatorships whose authority is new and unsupported by tradition, a system of state controls based on models inherited from Tsarist days has become tighter through the years. In the late twenties and early thirties, the Party membership was charged with the multiple roles of leadership, inspiration, checking accomplishment, and ferreting out slackness, failure, or treason. The task of the political police which was stressed was the liquidation of the remnants of the old regime, the members of the condemned classes who could not be absorbed into the new society and so had to be excised from it. Already dissenting socialists, anarchists, and peasants were included as targets. It was as if two societies lived side by side, the new, good, young Soviet Union, whose members were to be controlled not by physical force but by faith and discipline, and the remnants of the old, bad Tsarist society which had to be dealt with by the old political police methods. With a comrade, one reasoned, argued, or pled, but against one whose ancestry defined him as unredeemable the state used the old methods of arrest without trial followed by banishment or execution. The political police were themselves something foreign, headed by the Polish zealot, Dzerzhinski, whose motto was that it was better that one hundred innocent men die than one guilty one escape. Meanwhile, the struggle for dominance within the Party went on, and control of the political police became part of the struggle. The classification of "enemies of the people," once reserved for remnants of the old regime and for anti-Bolshevik parties, was extended to cover dissent within the Party, even while the legend grew that Lenin had warned that the Party must never pass a death sentence on one of its own members. The history of Stalin's rise to power, accurately mirrored in his accusations against Tito, is the history of a growing dependence on a form of administration within which the political police played a significant role. Today, the political police are an integral part of the ordinary governmental apparatus, with their own Party cells, responsible to the Central Committee and the Politburo to guard against their becoming independent of the Party. What the ordinary Party membership was earlier supposed to be—a single-mindedly devoted, incorruptible, ever-watchful, ruthless executive of the will of the Party—is now attributed to the political police (MVD-MGB). The political police now have a membership placed at somewhere over a million and a half, which includes frontier police and the administration of labor camps. They are placed strategically in every branch of Soviet life and are responsible for the security of the system and for defending it against sabotage and treason.

Informants' accounts show that, while the single-mindedness attributed to the political police is related to the demands made on Party members, they (the political police) are also felt to be predatory and alien. A DP informant reports on this attitude during the war:

Every worker of the political police is like a monk in a monastery because he is surrounded by his (svoi) people and has almost nothing in common with the surrounding society. They are like a wolf in the forest where there is always famine and seek food for themselves. . . . The political police do not go to balls or other public diversions but if there is a political meeting some place in the city or in the collective farm they appear there and look for something for themselves at this meeting. The political police always do their work at night and sleep in the daytime. . . . Here it should be emphasized that the political police worker is a very good family man and only does this because he sees an enemy of the people in every person and believes that every person carries in himself something or other hostile to the regime. His ideas are always imbued with this and therefore he lives with his wife and children distinctly better than all other citizens in the USSR.

Here we have the whole picture, the wolf who preys on the rest of society, but impersonally, because it is his task, and who receives rewards from the state which he protects.

A strong contrast is drawn between the venality in ordinary civilian affairs and the behavior of the political police:

As is known, everything in the Soviet Union can be bought for money—passports (travel authorizations), liberation from jail for stealing, speculation and similar crimes, but if one is taken into the hands of the political police then such things won't go for no one can buy them off. It might be said that this is because their business is known to many other political police and if one political police worker has to arrest someone, then the chiefs know about it, and one fears the other, therefore it is absolutely impossible to buy off the political police and liberate a political offender in these cases. [Reported by an informant who left the Soviet Union during the war.]

The fear that they inspire in all others is thus suggested as the sanction which keeps them incorruptible. Those who are fear-inspiring are also the most afraid. In the distinction which the informant draws between ordinary civil difficulties which can be settled and "cases which fall into the hands of the political police" can be seen a suggestion of a breakdown in the Soviet attempt to make every area of life equally political and sacred and every error of any sort into treason. Treason is here defined not by the act, but by which agency is called upon to punish the act. This is a further shift toward the disassociation of the criminal and the crime discussed earlier. The political police, charged with the arrest of a certain number of subversive people, prowl about among the populace (who are all considered in some degree to be guilty) and arbitrarily select particular victims. These thereupon, by definition, are no longer regarded as engaged in the minor law-breaking that is believed to be universally practiced and is ordinarily accepted as inevitable, but become "enemies of the people," traitors, saboteurs, wreckers, etc. The imputed impersonality of the whole procedure is illustrated by the belief that within the prison camps it was only necessary to have a given number of prisoners, so that a man could take another man's identity, answer to his name, and later escape without anyone being the wiser.

It is important to note, also, that while the Party member is expected to be stricter with himself and his fellow Party members than is a non-Party member, he is exhorted to maintain contact with his non-Party associates in factory and collective farm and by such contact to maintain his nearness to the masses and also his intimate knowledge of what is going on and so increase his power of manipulation. He is a part of a society which is meshed together. But the political police are meshed into the society only at the very top. Where the Party member draws at least part of his strength from the people, the political police draw their power from their *lack of association* with the rest of the population.

Where their foreignness was once emphasized by the number of non-Russians among them, today it is represented by the belief, expressed both by former members of the NKVD and by outsiders, that the ideal recruit for the political police is an orphan who has been reared in one of the institutions for homeless children. These children, utterly desolate and alone, are pictured as going out at night to steal from the local populace—all men are their enemies, but they are completely loyal to each other. With this ideal background—for we have no information on what proportion of the police are so recruited—they then become, both in the view of informants from inside and from outside, a group apart, specially privileged and immune to temptation and corruption.

Sometimes the political police, in making arrests, follow the particular occupational categories specified by the labor needs of the Soviet Union, as allowed for in the section called "banishment" (*asylka*) in the Penal Code of the Soviet Union. To Western eyes, an order to a division of political police that twenty carpenters must be included among those arrested during the next few months expresses a degree of cynicism which makes it seem impossible that anyone involved in the system could be left with a shadow of faith in the *bona fides* of the state. These practices are related to older Russian practices—to the varieties of services for which it was customary to draft men in the Moscow state, to the practice of moving the whole population of a village, and to the practice, during the reign of Peter the Great, of assigning whole villages to work in factories. They are also related to old attitudes toward police arrests, well expressed in the report of an informant: "The police just have to arrest somebody. If this one escapes they will arrest two more. So why do they have to have this [particular] one?" The belief held by the police, that everyone in the population is to some degree guilty, is supported by the actual fact that everyone is involved in some order of illegality, if not of active hostility toward the regime. These antecedents make the combination of labor recruiting and punishment for political crimes less unintelligible. Within many Christian communities it would not seem inappropriate to select at random someone to play Judas, for all are believed to have, to some degree, betrayed their Savior in their hearts. The fortunate will be chosen for the role of Saints, of which they are unworthy, and the unfortunate will be chosen for the role of Judas Iscariot, which to a degree unfairly emphasizes their unworthiness.

An unpublished manuscript,[152] based on detailed investigation of attitudes of Soviet people imprisoned during the purges, describes an even more extreme type of explanation:

> Why was the prophet Jonah thrown into the· sea? In order to find expiation and save all the rest. He was no more guilty than the rest, but it fell to his lot. The Soviet system cost the Russian people dear. Who paid for the famine of 1932 and 1933? Who should answer for all the sacrifices aroused by the imperfection of the system, errors in the plan, faults in the apparatus, inability of executives, etc. Those to whose lot it falls . . . [must answer]. In order to save the system as a whole, in order to divert the wrath of the people from its leaders, it is necessary to sacrifice millions of innocent persons. Furthermore they are only relatively innocent for every Soviet person bears greater or lesser accountability for Bolshevism as a whole and in its parts.

The existence of such attitudes, combined with the expectation of total mobilization of the general population at all times, which Western societies expect only during wartime, and the confusion between labor for the state and punishment taken together, makes it possible for a political police to become an integral part of the system, one which people can accept with resignation, as they might the sufferings from rain and snow which fall unequally upon a people all of whom are guilty. And the number of arrests which the political police make each month, each year, serves as confirmation to those higher up that a great deal of counterrevolutionary activity, espionage, and sabotage does exist, which confirmation is well supported by fulsome written confessions. That the confessions are fabrications does not matter.

In discussing the hypothesis that all of the population are to some degree guilty of acts and thoughts hostile to the regime, it is necessary to bear in mind the Bolshevik doctrine that every act is a political act, that the whole personality is involved in all acts so that one cannot be a good father and a bad cell secretary, and that nothing is a trifle—any act however small may lead to disaster.

In addition to these ideas of universal guilt, it is of course important to realize that agriculture and industry, the arts and sciences, as well as the army, the navy, and the ordinary Civil services are all matters of state. Add further that Bolshevik theory connects organization so closely with the Truth that, if the true Line is followed, the true organization is expected to be available to be applied, so that bureaucratic inefficiencies, faulty distribution of labor, untrained supervision, and even failure of a crop due to weather conditions can all be easily regarded or presented as being due to someone's political failure to follow accurately enough the right Line. Experience with rapid industrialization in which there is a shortage of almost every sort of skill has demonstrated, in other countries, that this is a difficult operation which in any case involves a great deal of waste of men and materials. Experience with the state operation of

---

[152] See footnote 38, p. 46.

large enterprises, in which the coercive power of government is combined with the particular attempts of an employer of labor to run a railroad or to build a ship, again has demonstrated how many administrative pitfalls exist. Both of these conditions, rapid industrialization which outstripped the capacity to produce trained personnel and governmental operation of large-scale enterprises over very wide areas, existed in the Soviet Union. And, in addition, organization and efficiency are treated as ideological as well as technical problems. The discussion of the working out of Bolshevik ideology in the administration of agriculture and industry will be limited to the way in which the theories of organization and accountability overstrain the whole system, producing conditions in which almost everyone is accountable for things outside his control, to the results of this diffusion of accountability in inefficiency and illegality, and to the punitive measures with which the state attempts to correct it. To illustrate the effects of this politicizing of technical activities, it will be useful to examine in some detail an informant's account of the way technical failure is handled politically:

> A collective farm had a contract with a Machine Tractor Station that the Machine Tractor Station would work 600 hectares of land, in the course of 36 days beginning on the 15th of June, and that if this contract was not fulfilled, the MTS would be held responsible and would have to pay the collective farm a forfeit for the loss. At the contracted time the MTS sent tractors which were only in nominal repair, so that they were out of commission most of the time. When they were repaired they were taken off the work and sent other places (in the same sort of nominal fulfillment). At the due date they had not worked the land, nor did they work it later, and the land of the collective farm remained unworked. The collective farm turned to the secretary of the district Party committee and stated that as the MTS had not completed its work, the collective farm could not fulfill its contract with the state.

Now up to this point the story might occur anywhere where there are division of labor, machines which may be inadequately repaired, and contracts with forfeiture clauses in them. But from now on the account assumes a distinctively Soviet character:

> The first act of the district committee was to call the collective farm to accountability for interrupting the state plan and the MTS was called to accountability for sabotage. In the court, the collective farm attempted to stand on its contract, but this was not recognized. The court simply established that the collective farm had not completed its supply of grain to the state, and for interrupting the state plan, the chairman of the collective farm and 3 brigadiers were given eight-year jail sentences, and the case of the MTS was turned over to the political police as sabotage and the director of the MTS and two of his brigadiers were sent to a labor camp, without further trial, with ten year sentences.

Here the original trouble was technical—unrepaired tractors—which was not necessarily even within the control of the MTS but may have been a failure of some central agency to supply parts or even to manufacture them.

Punctuality has been exceedingly difficult to instill into a population unused to regular hours, and heavy fines and jail sentences have been introduced on a drastic scale—for example, lateness of twenty-one minutes might mean a loss of a third of the salary or a three-month jail sentence. Arguments about broken-down transports are not accepted, for it is held that every worker should have left his home in time to walk to the factory in case every other means of transportation failed. This provision illustrates neatly the high level of moral devotion expected of each Soviet citizen, the absence of which can in itself constitute a punishable offense, and the stress on the control of individual behavior (lateness) by punishment where the real need is for an improvement of the transportation system.

Examination of the functioning of any large ministry, agriculture or industry, shows that there is a continuous conflict between the diffusion of accountability, which exceeds the power to control, and the consequent uncertainty as to which agencies are actually responsible for anything, combined with interference from one accountable agency in the affairs of other agencies, in an effort to prevent the failures or exposures which are likely to be so severely and so indiscriminately punished. There also seems to be little distinction between mandatory and permissive interference and verification by one agency in the affairs of another.

One sharp editorial points out[153] that "some shortsighted people think that the execution of the threshing of the harvest is the affair of the collective farm," and adds that the MTS director should remember that he bears personal accountability for carrying out the grain threshing. A second[154] declares that "the capacity of the village Party organization to conduct mass political work among the masses is verified by the harvest and grain deliveries." This means that a secretary of a collective farm Party organization would supplement the work of a collective farm chairman by making personal observations of the threshing activities, investigating how much time was wasted for lunch, and raising these questions at general meetings, thus changing "the atmosphere" and introducing "a spirit of anxiety and self-criticism."[155] When it was further discovered that a grain dryer was needed, "the Party organization took this objective under its control, the Communists of the construction brigade were commissioned to prepare materials and particular Communists were commissioned to find equipment." The editorial then adds: "Having received concrete tasks people felt responsible."

On a collective farm, however, there is not only a management commission under the leadership of the chairman, but also a revision commission, which

---

[153] "Grain to the Government on Time," from *Sotsialisticheskoe Zemledelie* (Socialist Agriculture), August 17, 1948.

[154] S. Bardin, "The Kolkhoz Party Organization in the Harvest Days," from *Sotsialisticheskoe Zemledelie*, August 15, 1949.

[155] "The Secretary of the Kolkhoz Party Organization," from *Sotsialisticheskoe Zemledelie*, August 10, 1948.

must conduct an "unrelenting struggle with mismanagement in the collective," but "without interfering in the work of the management and without becoming a substitute for it."[156]

Furthermore, the Party is involved in what is taking place in the collective farms at every level. For example, a decree about sowing was issued jointly by the Council of Ministers of the USSR and the chief Party Secretary of the All-Union Communist Party. On the county level, we find such interference as the refusal of a county Party committee to permit the chairman of a collective farm to remove or replace a link leader without its permission. But this involvement of the Party organizations in the details of administration in particular collective farms is explicable, as the Party committee officials may be held accountable for anything that goes wrong. In one case, upper-level Party organizations put the blame for backwardness and poor production of a group of collective farms on the lower-level Party organizations and dissolved one hundred and fifty of them. If skilled operators of agricultural combines are working in the wrong place, it is because the Party has not concerned itself with the "political and cultural growth of the combine operators."

Not only is the Party, at all levels, involved, but the ordinary executive organs of government are also involved and accountable if the collective farms do not make correct use of their capital funds or fail to contribute their seeds to the special seed reserves.

It must be stressed again that these multiplications of functions and agencies are not distinctive of the Soviet Union. It is possible to find instances in United States agriculture where ten or fifteen agencies are attempting to improve the functioning of a set of farmers in one community. The significant difference lies in the degree of accountability and in the way in which the officials of each agency, at each level, may be held totally accountable for events over which they have little or no control. We only need to add the belief that punishment in some degree implies some kind of guilt to picture a situation in which the alternatives are apathetic lack of initiative—for which one may be punished, for this is sabotage—and officious attempts to control the situation, which may also be stigmatized as misplaced interference and punished with demotion or worse.

If the management of a plant or the chairman of a collective farm and the Party Secretary do not get along together, there is possibility of endless friction with each jockeying for control and calling on associations higher up in his respective political hierarchy, a jockeying which is time-consuming and which lowers efficiency. If it ends in a victory for one or the other, this only inaugurates another struggle after the loser is replaced. The usual solution in American life would be to try to work out an understanding between the two men, both

---

[156] "Public Control in the Kolkhoz," from *Sotsialisticheskoe Zemledelie*, June 25, 1948.

of whom must bear accountability for what goes on. But this again is reprehensible and makes them guilty of the political sin of "family relations."

Stalin in 1937 said:[157]

> To select workers correctly means to select workers according to objective criteria of business and suitability, not according to accidental, subjective, narrow and personal criteria. Most frequently so-called acquaintances are chosen, personal friends, fellow townsmen, people who have shown personal devotion, masters of eulogies to their patrons, irrespective of whether they are suitable from a political and practical standpoint. . . . In such family conditions there is no place for self-criticism of work by the leaders. Naturally, such family conditions create a favorable environment for the nurture of reptiles, not Bolsheviks.

In the struggles between the two, the director or chairman—who in a great many cases today is also a Party member—and the Party Secretary, each is forced into the struggle, not necessarily by personal ambition but because each is accountable.

In the postwar fiction, there is an interesting reaction to the Party doctrine that failure to achieve in production or agriculture is politically sinful. This is the development of the character of the very successful engineer-manager who during the war learned how to get things done, using a variety of dubious methods, and who bases his self-respect on his positive value to the state. If it is sinful not to achieve, to fail for whatever reason, then, flows the logic which underlies these characters such as Kondrashev[158] and Listopad,[159] it is virtuous to succeed by whatever means. The fictional stories of these characters, as well as interviews with recent émigrés and earlier experiences of Soviet industry and agriculture, support the contention that the system is such that the most conscientious, the most enterprising and genuinely devoted executive is forced into a great number of evasions of the law, into dodges and devices and illegal mutual agreements in order to keep his enterprise running and to fulfill his contract with the state, for the nonfulfillment of which he and many others in far parts of the Soviet Union may suffer severe penalties. Whether it be the device by which a village store with clothes for sale refuses to sell for anything except eggs because the county was short on its egg delivery to the government, or the more complicated operations in which managers of big plants exchange supplies extralegally in order to keep their plants running, a great deal of wangling, scrounging, and arranging is needed to keep any Soviet enterprise functioning. It is even possible to publish a novel[160] representing collective

---

[157] J. Stalin, *Mastering Bolshevism,* Report to the 1937 Plenum of the Central Committee of the CPSU, printed in *Bol'shevik,* April 1, 1937.

[158] K. Simonov, "The Smoke of the Fatherland" (*Dym otechestva*), *Novyi Mir,* November, 1947.

[159] V. Panova, "Kruzhilikha," *Znamya,* November–December, 1947.

[160] A. Subbotin, *The Rank and File (Prostye Liudi),* Moscow, 1948.

farm life in idyllic terms, in which the heroine, chairman of the collective farm, succeeds in getting tractors for her fields at the expense of another collective farm because the director of the MTS is in love with her.

Within such a system—in which exist pull, bribery, mutual condonement of illegal actions, back-scratching, and wire pulling, all of which may be branded at any moment as "family relations," sabotage, or treason—there is obviously room for a great deal of petty theft, graft, and corruption, in which the conscientious and enterprising are joined with the venal and dishonest in a sort of strange collaboration which must increase, in the most devoted and hard working, the sense of being involved in political sinfulness. This type of alliance is represented in fiction in the similarities attributed to the successful, upper-level people, who are hard-headedly able to pursue success, and to the "lower depths," the completely extralegal people who flourish in the forbidden channels of illegal trade.[161]

The press periodically nags, scolds, and reports cases of heavy sentence passed on individual peasants for particular thefts, but the atmosphere seems to be one, if not of condonement, of at least a resigned acceptance of the fact that there is nothing to be done about the general conditions. Informants' accounts suggest a considerable development of elaborate accommodation devices, of which only one example will be given—from an informant who had been a doctor in a hospital in Vladivostok. When the informant went to this post,

> his first patient came in and asked for a statement of illness. When the doctor wished to examine him he was greatly surprised. "Don't you know our custom?" he said. "We pay a fixed price for a statement. I have to earn some money. When you give me a statement, I shall go to the market place and try to earn some money buying and selling." Since the doctor refused to issue a false report, the worker went to the chief of the hospital, complaining. After work the young doctor was called in to the chief and was told that if he behaved this way there was no place for him in the hospital and besides the workers would beat him up. The reprimand was made in very general terms. The doctor was told he was preventing people from making a living.

This last statement, used as justification for the illegality, harks back to a deep-rooted Russian attitude, found in the old *mir*, that every human being has a right to a living, a right which carries a kind of sanction of its own.

If full accommodation is to be reached between a governmental system which depends on terror and on mass or indiscriminate arrest and punishment rather than on techniques of administration which make it possible to limit and fix responsibility and the populace who are subjected to this terror, then what is required is an attitude toward the political police which reflects the general acceptance of illegality—something comparable to the American attitude toward traffic regulations about parking in a large city in which almost everyone breaks the rules and does not report his neighbor for breaking them. No systematic

---

[161] Analyzed in detail as background for this report by Vera Schwarz (Alexandrova).

attempt is made by the police to stop the practice completely, but periodically there will be a great outburst of activity—a mass of tickets, fines, and summonses, which do not arouse undue resentment in those who get the summonses, they were just unlucky, that's all; and it's not the fault of the police—the streets were getting unbearably crowded, and obviously the police had to put on a show. In such a situation no one can feel unjustly treated, even though only a few hundred offenders may be singled out while guilty thousands go untouched. All are guilty and periodically some must be punished.

For such an attitude to develop in the Soviet Union, it would be necessary for the police to be regarded as impersonally as they were in the case described by an informant on page 91 (who saw them merely as wolves who must eat someone) and for the harshness of the punishments to be considerably mitigated. An account of an ex-White army officer and professor, who had worked faithfully for the Party for many years and was then accused of being a spy as his past seemed to lend color to the charge and make it difficult to refute, describes how he was kept in jail for a long time while an attempt was made to get a confession from him:

> The old professor said that if he had had some enemies he would have named them, but he had none. They would have let the professor go, but they had already held him too long and could not explain why they had held him so long if nothing was wrong.

In this account there is the underlying assumption that "it's just the system and no one is to blame."

But any assumption that the system rather than the individual is to blame runs completely contrary to Bolshevik moral doctrine, which, although insisting on an inescapable connection between an economic system and the over-all behavior of individuals within it, nevertheless holds the individual Party member or citizen to be completely accountable and does not allow any trifling slip to be overlooked. By holding everyone accountable for every slightest act, by holding all persons in responsible positions accountable for much that is due to the poor organization or administration for which they are not really responsible, the Bolsheviks create a system within which not responsible moral behavior, rigid correctness, nor meticulous honesty form the behavior which enables a man to survive, but in which a premium is placed upon the individual who can keep his head above water by devious means. The very extremity and exaggeration of their political moral demands are self-defeating by creating a political form which fails to reward those who take the demands seriously.

It is necessary to take the age of individual Soviet citizens carefully into account in making any judgment on trends in the Soviet Union. To the extent that the condoning and collaborative behavior occurs among the middle-aged and older, it may be regarded possibly as a residue of old-experienced attitudes of evasion and sabotage current in Tsarist Russia. This would still mean, however, that Soviet youth are exposed in the schools and youth organizations to one kind of official indoctrination and meet quite a different kind of behavior at every turn in their daily lives. The degree of contrast felt by the young between Bolshevik moral indoctrination and the real world of political dishonesty and evasion would then be one factor in the selection, from youth groups, of those who are most able to make the necessary moral compromises.

This study has concerned itself with attitudes toward authority, with the conduct models which are officially presented in the Soviet Union, and with informal and indirect evidence of the way in which actual practice diverges from these models. With such a framework, very little mention has been made of a subject which is, however, crucial to an understanding of the Soviet Union, that is, promises made by the regime of tangible material improvement and the extent to which these promises have been fulfilled. The major goal which Bolshevism has offered has been that of the good society in which, within an institutional framework where there would be neither exploitation of man by man nor domination of man over man, there would be abundance in which all would share. The realization of such a society is dependent on the actual existence of food, clothing, housing, and medical and educational facilities adequate for and available to the entire population. The inducements offered during the first Five-Year Plan to postpone the enjoyment of these material blessings for a few years in order to bring the good society nearer resulted in disappointment when the promises were not fulfilled.

Such experiences as that of Britain during World War II suggest that it is easier to induce a people to endure physical hardships in the name of values such as freedom and justice, sharing equally the burdens of abstinence and deprivation, than it is to induce one generation to go without butter so that the next generation can have it. In addition to failure to produce enough consumer goods to meet the expectations it had aroused, the Soviet regime, in order to strengthen its power, resorted to the device of giving differential access to the scarce consumer goods (1) by direct premium and prize giving, (2) by discriminatory rationing, and (3) by wage scales combined with special access to scarce or specially priced consumer goods. Higher officials have long been given special privileges. The expectation of loyalty of the political police today is calculated—in addition to a reliance upon the solidarity which comes from the risks and rewards of their being a group set apart from the population and with great power—on their being given economic privileges so great as to place them beyond ordinary temptation. From a Western point of view, the regime has been trapped in an abuse of its own value system by an attempt to approach the ideal of an equalization of material wealth by the creation of gross inequalities. From the Bolshevik point of view, however, which does not recognize this kind of connection between ends and means and regards any means as possibly appropriate to any end, this is merely a necessary detour in the approach to the perfect society.

One effort which the regime has made through the years to deal with the discrepancies between ideal and actuality, between promise and fulfillment, has been official insistence upon the superiority of material and of health and welfare service for the majority of people inside the Soviet Union as compared with the conditions of the majority of people in Western countries. Coercive measures since the war have been directed toward the danger that any large proportion of the population might discover, as a result of the experience abroad of Soviet troops or from Western propaganda, that the material conditions of the majority of the peoples of the Western countries are not, as the regime has pictured them, inferior to those in the Soviet Union but are actually better. This fear has been expressed in the rigid censorship on news, in suspicion of all those who have been abroad, and in the campaign against cringing before the West. It suggests that statements about relative conditions in the East and West have been such conscious falsifications that loyalty of the citizen is expected to flag and fail when confronted by evidence of workers' houses in Germany or by food conditions in Rumania. The harshness of the measures with which the regime combats any diffusion of knowledge about conditions in the West suggests that this fear can only be reduced if material conditions in the Soviet Union can be steadily and appreciably improved. But this possibility is rendered unlikely because the Bolshevik dogma that they are encircled by hostile enemies all crouching to attack makes it expedient to divert such a large part of Soviet manpower and resources into military operations that there is not the margin available for improvement. Yet without this improvement, the present fear of the top leadership, that knowledge of the real contrasts between East and West will reach and subvert the people, increases the severity of the measures which must be taken against a potentially treasonable population filled with potential wreckers and saboteurs and so diminishes the possibility of any relaxing of the controls exercised by the political police. There is, of course, evidence of considerable relaxation after the excesses of the late thirties but not sufficient to make it likely that the present level of police supervision will decrease.

Chapter 7

POSSIBLE DEVELOPMENTS IN THE SOVIET UNION

Let us assume that conditions in the Soviet Union remain somewhat as they are with (1) a steady belief in military threat from the West keeping up expenditures on armaments and so preventing the standard of living from rising, with (2) a continuing fear of the impact of news of the higher standard of living in the West producing disloyalty, keeping the feeling of need of tight police controls high, with (3) the tightness, harshness, and indiscriminateness of the police controls producing a general situation in which almost everyone, except the political police themselves, is involved in political crime of some sort, and with (4) a continuance of the system of moral-political education in the schools and youth organizations which is designed to build a strong individual conscience, strongly motivated by an exacting standard of devoted political behavior incompatible with an atmosphere of condonement, evasion, and general political corruption. We may then consider certain weaknesses or points of conflict in the system which are suggested by the particular material which has been analyzed in this report.

Two areas of weakness, related to the contrasts between the officially expressed ideals of the Bolsheviks and the actual coercive terroristic police state with its accompaniment of accommodation and corruption, may be identified.

1. Weakness in the area of leadership. The recruitment of youth for positions of responsibility and leadership may be most adversely affected by the inability of those who develop the desired strong individual conscience and high idealism to survive within the system of political dishonesty. Those who survive in a system in which there is such a strong contrast between the ideal and the actual practice are likely to be lacking in the very qualities of moral devotion and initiative which are necessary for the future development of Soviet society. To the extent that particular areas of Soviet life are relatively freer from the type of political pressure which interferes with any disinterested attempt to do a job well—as has been the case in the Soviet army at some periods—they may become relatively better staffed and more efficient than other areas. Such discrepancies may in turn put strains upon the system or provoke reprisals from other more politicized areas.

2. Weaknesses in the masses of the people. A diminution in the enthusiasm and available energy of the population may be the consequence of the methods used to preserve the security of the regime by the political police, whose incorruptibility is partly based, not on a moral-political faith, however fanatical, but on fear and the prestige derived from the disproportionate share of material goods and services which are placed at their disposal. In practice, this means that the group to whom the security of the system is entrusted are seen by the populace as being motivated by fear rather than by faith and as being treated by the state as if they were so lacking in innate devotion that, unless the rewards given by the state outdistance their possible underground methods of "self-supply" (*samosnabzhenia*), their loyalty cannot be relied upon. Popular feeling about these contradictions may accentuate the harshness and indiscriminateness of the police measures, since the police seek to counteract the fears of the regime concerning their reliability. But increased terroristic practices should weaken the feeling of the populace that where there is punishment there must be some guilt. In addition, Soviet methods of child rearing and education may reduce the tendency of the individual to feel guilty of the crime which he has committed only in imagination, now an important condition making for some acceptance of the terroristic methods of the political police.

A populace disillusioned regarding the hope of tangible rewards, subjected to terroristic pressure, living within a situation in which all are treated as suspect —and most of all those who must also be the most incorruptible—may become steadily less responsive to positive motivation, more apathetic, and less able to participate with any enthusiasm in Soviet life. The Soviet Union, however, has relied heavily on compensating for organizational inefficiency and for the gaps between plan and fulfillment by tapping the energies of the people and by such devices as correcting for a faulty budget for a given enterprise by whipping up the workers to the voluntary contribution of extra hours. A reduction in the availability of such energy in the population as the people react to loss of hope and increasing sharp controls administered by those who are seen as living on the fat of the land should lower the productivity of the system and its capacity to meet new strains and difficulties.

An examination of the great discrepancies between ideal and actuality, between Bolshevik Party ideal and Soviet State practice, discrepancies which are accentuated by the system of education under which everyone under forty-five has now been educated, therefore suggests that a loss of leadership personnel and an increase in apathy in the general population are two strong possible weaknesses of the Soviet authority system as it is currently inculcated and administered.

An increasing *strength* and *stability* within the Soviet Union would involve the following conditions: (1) a lessening of the fear of the top leadership of the imminence of capitalist attack, which lessening did not involve too much accompanying open struggle for power at the top; (2) a relaxation of the political police controls which reflect the fear of a population whose standard of living is kept low by armaments; (3) the development, in the political police themselves and throughout the entire bureaucracy, of sharper theories of function and responsibility accompanied by methods of detecting actual criminals; (4) the setting up of workable channels of authority within organizations; and (5) a growing closeness of fit between punishment and real guilt on the one hand and reward and real virtue, as virtues are outlined in the schools, on the other. Such a development is dependent (1) in part on world conditions, (2) in part on accidents of leadership within the Soviet Union, and (3) in part on the extent to which engineering and scientific training is likely to be reflected in increasing capacity for realistic organization. If, however, all of these conditions should come about, one might then predict that there might be a strong puritanical tone to the society.[162] In the light of our contemporary knowledge of the relationship between moral training and character, this would produce a population which, while better disciplined than the present Soviet population, might also be lacking in the reserves of zest and energy which the present population displays.

These alternatives are not, of course, exclusive of other possibilities, but they are strongly suggested by this body of material and should be taken seriously into account in planning research and in contemporary propaganda plans as well as in longer-term estimates of the strength of the Soviet Union.

---

[162] A full description of the basis for this statement is beyond the scope of the present report.

APPENDIX A

ABSTRACT OF RESEARCH ON LEADERSHIP IN SOVIET AGRICULTURE AND THE COMMUNIST PARTY

A separate, full-length RAND report will soon be issued on problems of *Leadership in Soviet Agriculture and the Communist Party*. This study, by H. S. Dinerstein, was conducted as part of Studies in Soviet Culture. It is a comprehensive analysis of the morale-producing and morale-destroying features of Soviet agricultural organization.

Based on printed Soviet written materials and on interviews and private documents obtained from ex-Soviet citizens, the study presents a detailed analysis of the organization of the kolkhoz, its systems of incentives, the relations of the Machine Tractor Stations to the kolkhoz, and the role of county and province agriculture authorities in planning on local levels.

The difficulties of meeting unrealistically planned quotas and the techniques of evading responsibility for nonfulfillment are presented in considerable detail. The economic consequences of unrealistic planning, falsification of records, bribery, and personal profiteering are described. The responsibility of Party and government officials and the attempted control, enforcement, and punishment procedures are related to the effects on farm-worker morale, described in a setting which takes account of the historical development of collective farming, the psychology of the Russian peasant, and the political institutions of the Soviet system.

APPENDIX B

SUMMARY OF CONCLUSIONS OF RESEARCH ON SOVIET CHILD TRAINING IDEALS AND THEIR POLITICAL SIGNIFICANCE

(Conducted as part of Studies in Soviet Culture)

BY E. CALAS

From the earlier official attitude, which reflected the belief that socialist iety would take upon itself in full the upbringing of children, the Soviet vernment has shifted to an emphasis on the significant role of the family l family upbringing of children. Recent laws, decrees, and public announcents of leaders encourage the growth of a closely knit family and of parental hority. From the strengthened and united family the state expects full peration in the matter of molding "the moral countenance" of future Soviet zens. Parents are held totally responsible for mental attitudes which they wittingly or unwittingly transfer to their children; they are called on to examine their own attitudes and behavior and to struggle against possible carry-overs (*perezhitki*) from the capitalist past. Parents must serve as models of political and social activity, industriousness, unselfishness, and optimism. This will guarantee them the love and respect of their children. Children become emotionally alienated from parents who do not act in accordance with the precepts and ideals which the children learn in school and in the Pioneer or Komsomol organization.

In relation to children, parents must be unremittingly vigilant, exacting, and consistent in disciplinary demands and in the imposition of duties; no relaxation of effort on the parents' part is permissible for fear that the child may fall under bad influence and be controlled by antisocial elements. While parents should show warmth, affection, and understanding, they should not permit excessive intimacy, which might undermine their authority. Parents must not be all-forgiving, for conduct deviations in children cannot be tolerated. Parental indulgence interferes with proper upbringing and turns a child into a despot at home and into a difficult child in the school collective. The ideal parents are little differentiated as to their function in relation to the child, the father being encouraged to assume equal responsibility with the mother in the matter of upbringing.

Upbringing must develop in children the qualities of personality which, combined, form the moral countenance of a future fighter for communism: ideological purposefulness, strong convictions, patriotism, sense of duty, courage, endurance, tenacity, self-control, humanism, vigor, industriousness, optimism, generosity combined with the care of property, modesty, neatness, politeness, and sensitivity to the needs of others. Obedience is seen as the first step toward developing a disciplined will. Anxiety related to performance of duty is viewed as a virtue. Qualities are regarded as virtues if they are socially oriented; they are undeserving of approval when used to further purely personal interests. Training from early infancy is recommended; constancy of effort on a child's part and the carrying through of any undertaking to the end receive heavy stress. The will to overcome obstacles must replace the intolerable tendency to follow the line of least resistance. Most related "noncompulsive" behavior is ascribed to the influence of the past through the medium of faulty family relations and attitudes. The planned transformation of man is rationalized by the concept of the moral betterment of man: "The process of remaking man which is taking place under the influence of socialistic conditions, as well as the creation of a new man, must attract the exclusive attention of Soviet pedagogy." It is admitted that the process of forming the new morality involves a difficult and tense struggle.

In all circumstances, personal interests must be subordinated to collective ones. The desirability of a large family is stressed because it affords the child his first experience of collective life, accustoming him to respect older siblings and to give succor to the younger. From an early age a child should be trained in a feeling of responsibility to the collective and in upholding the honor of the group (his class, or Pioneer brigade). The child should be trained to value highly the approval of the collective and to fear its disapproval. "The rules of conduct adopted by the collective become binding on the member, and finally one's sense of responsibility to the collective becomes the basis of self-evaluation." While it is one's duty to confess errors and misdeeds, to accept criticism with respect and without offense, and to subordinate oneself to the demands of the collective, the moral gain for the culprit is placed in the foreground: "Courage is developed by the need always to say the truth, not to commit dishonorable, amoral deeds, and, if such are committed, courageously to recognize one's guilt before the collective and its leader, to submit to the condemnation of the misdeed and to become imbued with the determination to mend it." The emphasis is not on the cathartic release of guilt feelings but on moral growth. Adults may enlist the disapproval of a child's peers or may delegate authority so that corrective action comes from the child's collective. Organized collective (such as the Pioneer organization) may instigate corrective action independently by resorting to group accusation. While the role of comradeship and friendship is extolled, solidarity with the collective is placed above personal feelings of friendship. While interpersonal relations are generally approved, there is always the conditional factor: personal relations must fit into the required pattern, that is, they must serve the ultimate strengthening of the state.

Correct discipline should lead gradually to self-discipline. Every influence of the adult on the child, be it of encouragement or punishment, has as its aim the molding of the child's behavior, interests, views, and impulses, and the development of the convictions which will determine his future conduct. There is consistent emphasis on punishment as correction rather than as retribution. The nature of a misdeed dictates the handling of it, and when punishment is indicated it must fit the concrete circumstances of each case. Parents and teachers must be aware of the "point of application" of their educational influence (*vozdeistvie*), which requires an understanding of a child's motivations in committing a deed. There are frequent warnings against an abuse of punishment and scolding as well as of praise and reward, because through repetition they lose their effectiveness. An "eye to eye" talk is a recommended corrective measure which must be carried out when both the adult and the child are calm, because an adult's raised, irritated voice throws the child into either a state of sharp excitation or of inhibition. All forms of verbal reaction must be controlled, and in no event may they be used as catharses for adult feelings. Corporal punishment is outlawed, and other forms are warned against. Irony and humbling of arrogance are resorted to in cases of inadequate performance or bragging. A recommended punishment is the withholding of a treat, but this may not involve food. Repeated misdeeds which reveal bad traits of character and distorted concepts call for starting anew all the work with the child, and it is recommended that in the first place the parent place himself "under the microscope" to see in what way he himself has been inadequate to his task.

Sources used by E. Calas in research on Soviet Child Training Ideals and Their Political Significance.

An editorial, "Education in Comradeship and Friendship," *Family and School* (*Sem'ya i Shkola*), No. 4, 1948.
An editorial, "Training in Sense of Duty," *Family and School*, No. 6, 1948.
"From the Notes of a Teacher," *Family and School*, Nos. 7–8, 1946.
"Report on a Conference on Moral Education," *Family and School*, Nos. 4–5, 1946.
An editorial, "Training in Purposefulness," *Family and School*, No. 3, 1948.
An editorial, "Training in Courage," *Family and School*, No. 2, 1948.
An editorial, "On Cheerfulness and *Joie-de-vivre*," *Family and School*, No. 5, 1948.
An editorial, "Training in Endurance," *Family and School*, No. 1, 1948.
Alekseyev, A., and M. Andreyeva, "Report of a Working Mother," *Family and School*, No. 4, 1948.
Arkin, E. A., *Letters on the Upbringing of Children*, Uchpedgiz, 1940.
Bershanskaya, E. D., "After the War," *Family and School*, Nos. 4–5, 1946.
Bobovskaya, E., and N. Chetunova, "Problems of the Family and Morality," *Oktyabr'*, No. 1, 1948.

Dogvalevskaya, A. I., "A Congenial Family," *Family and School,* No. 3, 1947.

Glazounova, E. I., "Experience in Pioneer Work," *Soviet Pedagogy (Sovetskaia Pedagogika),* No. 5, 1948.

Golosnitskaya, N., *My Work in Upbringing of Children,* Uchpedgiz, 1948.

Goncharov, N. K., *Foundations of Pedagogy* (Chap. VIII, "Foundations of Moral Education"), Uchpedgiz, 1947.

Katina, L. P., "Laying the Foundations of Cultural Behavior in Kindergarten," *Pre-School Education (Doshkol'noe Vospitanie),* No. 6, 1948.

Kolbanovsky, V. N., Prof., "Ideological-Political Education in the Family," *Family and School,* No. 10, 1947.

———, "For the Further Strengthening of the Soviet Family," *Family and School,* No. 11, 1947.

Kononenko, Elena, "The Rope," *Family and School,* No. 6, 1948.

Kornilov, K. N., "Role of the Family in the Rearing of Pre-School Children," *Pre-School Education,* No. 7, 1948.

Likhacheva, N. F., "Mother-Tutoress," *Family and School,* No. 3, 1948.

Liublinskaya, A. A., "On the Misdeeds of Children," *Family and School,* No. 1, 1948.

Mahova, K. V., *Notebook of a Mother,* Academy of Pedagogical Sciences, 1948.

Makarenko, A. S., *Book For Parents,* Gospolitizdat, 1937 (out of print), Academy of Pedagogical Sciences, 1949.

———, Lecture on the *Book For Parents,* given in 1938, published in *Family and School,* No. 11, 1948.

Pechernikova, I. A., *Teaching the Schoolboy to Share in the Family Work,* Uchpedgiz, 1948.

Perel and Lyubimova, *The Legal Position of the Child in the Family,* Introduction, Uchpedgiz, 1932.

Perel (ed.), *Property Rights of Children,* Uchpedgiz, 1932.

Pisareva, L. V., "The Word in Upbringing," *Family and School,* Nos. 4–5, 1946.

Prozorov, G. C., Prof., "A. S. Makarenko on Pedagogical Tact in Family Upbringing," *Family and School,* No. 8, 1948.

Raskin, L. E., "Discipline and Culture in the Conduct of School Children," *Young Guard,* 1941.

———, "High-School Students in the Family," *Family and School,* No. 6, 1948.

Sapirstein, L., "School Director E. V. Mart'ianova," *Family and School,* No. 3, 1947.

Sergeyeva, A. D., "Love and Obligation to a Mother," *Family and School,* No. 11, 1947.

Simson, T. P., Dr., *Nervousness in Children and Measures for Preventing It,* Izd. Mosoblispolkoma, Zdravotdel, 1932.

Smirnov, V. E., "Absent-Mindedness and the Struggle Against It," *Family and School,* Nos. 4–5, 1946.

Speransky, G. N., *The Young Child,* Zdravotdel, 1941.

Svadkovsky, I. F., Prof., "Training in Obedience, Politeness and Modesty," *Family and School,* No. 3, 1947.

Sverdlov, G. M., *Marriage and the Family,* Uchpedgiz, 1946.

Syrkina, V. E., "Dreams and Ideals of Children," *Family and School,* No. 9, 1947.

Tadevosian, V. S., "Rights and Obligations of Parents in the Soviet State," stenogram of a lecture read in Moscow, May 29, 1947.

Usova, A. P., "On Ideology in Educational Work of Kindergartens," *Pre-School Education,* No. 5, 1948.

Yudina, N. V., "Parental Authority," *Family and School,* Nos. 4–5, 1946.

Zhdanov, A., "Report on the Magazines *Zvezda* and *Leningrad,*" Gospolitizdat, 1946, p. 36.

PERIODICALS

The 1947–1949 issues of the following magazines were read (but not including every issue, nor every item in any issue):

Novyi Mir (*New World*)
Oktyabr', (*October*)
Zvezda (*Star*)
Znamya (*Banner*)
Krokodil (*Crocodile*)
Zhurnal Moskovskovo Patriarkhata (*Journal of the Moscow Patriarchate*)
Sovetskaya Pedagogika (*Soviet Pedagogy*)
Murzilka
Vozhatyi (*Leaders*)
Pioner (*Pioneer*)
Doshkol'noe Vospitanie (*Pre-School Education*)
Soviet Woman
Literatura v Shkole (*Literature in Schools*)
Pediatria (*Pediatry*)
Nevropatologiia i Psykhiatriia (*Neuropathology and Psychiatry*)

NEWSPAPERS

Komsomol'skaia Pravda
Pionerskaya Pravda
Uchitel'skaya Gazeta (*The Teachers' Gazette*)
Morskoi Flot (*The Navy*)

BOOKS

Of the thirty-five juvenile books read, the following were intensively studied:
Gaidar, A., *Timur and his Band* (*Timur y yevo komanda*), Detgiz, 1940.
———, *Timur's Oath* (*Klyatva Timura*), Detgiz, 1941.
———, *Snow Fortress* (*Komandant smizhnoy kreposti*), Detgiz, 1945.
Kassil, L., *Chernysh, Brother of a Hero* (*Chernysh brat geroya*), Detgiz, 1938.
Kalma, N., *Copy Book of Andrei Sazonov* (*Tetrad' Andreya Sazonova*), Detgiz, 1948.
Voronkova, L., *Little Girl from the City* (*Devochka iz goroda*), Detgiz, 1943.
Teplitskaya, L., *In Our Yard* (*O nas vo dvore*), 1940 Handbook for Pioneer Leaders (*Vozhatyi*) in *Young Guard* (*Molodaya Gvardia*).
Fraerman, R., *The Far Voyage* (*Dal'nee plavanie*), Detgiz, 1946.
Ilina, Elena, *Fourth Height* (*Chetvertaya vysota*), Detgiz, 1948.
Paustovskii, K., *Summer Days* (*Letnie dni*), Detizdat, 1937.
Likstanov, I., *Nalyshok,* Detgiz, 1948.
Oseyeva, V., *Vasek Trubachev,* Detgiz, 1947.
Kurochkin, V., *Brigade of the Smart* (*Brigada smyshlennykh*), *Oktyabr'* (*October*), No. 9, 1947.
Kaverin, V., *Two Captains* (*Dva kapitana*), *Young Guard* (*Molodaya Gvardia*), 1947.
Dekhtereva, B. (ed.), *We Studied in Moscow* (*My uchilis' v Moskva*), Detgiz, 1947.
Nevskii, V., *The Bright Road* (*Svetlaya doroga*), *Young Guard* (*Molodaya Gvardia*), 1948.

From about thirty recently published adult novels, the following were examined closely:
Lifshitz, V., *Petrogradskaya Storona, New World* (*Novyi Mir*), Nos. 10–11, 1946.
Fedin, K., *First Joys* (*Pervye Radosti*), *New World* (*Novyi Mir*), Nos. 4–9, 1945.

Koptyayeva, A., *Comrade Anna (Tovarishch Anna)*, *Oktyabr'*, May, 1946.
Denison, I., *Pure Love (Chistaya liubov')*, *Oktyabr'*, No. 6, 1946.
Katerli, E., *The Stozharovs (Stozharovi)*, *Sovietski Pisatel' (Soviet Writer)*, 1948.
Bessonov, Y., *Maria (Maria)* in collection *Sudden Turn (Neozhidannyi povorot)*, *Sovietski Pisatel' (Soviet Writer)*, 1948.
Gausner, J., *We are Home Again (Vot my i doma)*, *Sovietski Pisatel' (Soviet Writer)*, 1948.
Voronin, S., *On Their Land (Na svoi zemle)*, *Sovietski Pisatel' (Soviet Writer)*, 1948.
Karaveyeva, A., *Running Start (Razbeg)*, *Sovietski Pisatel' (Soviet Writer)*, 1948.
Platonov, A., *Ivanov's Family (Sem'ya Ivanova)*, *Novyi Mir (New World)*, Nos. 10–11, 1946.
Perventsev, A., *Honor from the Days of Youth (Chest' S molodu)*, *Sovietski Pisatel' (Soviet Writer)*, 1949.
Panova, V., *Kruzhilikha*, *Sovietski Pisatel' (Soviet Writer)*, 1948.
Gerasimova, V., *Age Mates (Sverstnitsy)*, *Sovietski Pisatel' (Soviet Writer)*, 1948.

APPENDIX C

SUMMARY OF CONCLUSIONS OF RESEARCH ON PARTY AND NON-PARTY ORGANIZATIONS IN SOVIET INDUSTRY

BY L. H. HAIMSON

The summary conclusions presented here stem from a study of the structure and functioning of Soviet industrial organization, largely as viewed by members of the Soviet elite. Attention is focused, in this analysis, on the rationale which underlies the coexistence of Party and non-Party organs at various hierarchical levels of the industrial apparatus and on the changing interaction among these organs during the last decade.

Two levels of abstraction were observed in our examination of Soviet writings on industrial organization and were consequently adhered to in the analysis. We distinguished a body of pure theory, from which was derived a set of general politico-psychological assumptions concerning the relation of human personality to leadership and administrative supervision, and a level of applied theory as exemplified by the structure of the industrial apparatus and its expected functioning. Our examination of the practical difficulties which arise out of conflicts and contradictions inherent within the industrial system constituted a third level of analysis.

For the three facets of the study a wide variety of sources was used: In our examination of the theory of leadership and administration we drew upon authoritative texts of political theory and administrative law, keynote speeches and resolutions at the Party Congress of 1939 and at the Party Conference of 1941, editorials and articles in *Pravda* and *Bol'shevik* since 1939, and various authoritative pamphlets on this topic. For information concerning the structure and expected functioning of Party and non-Party planning, administrative and control organs in industry, we also drew on studies by Soviet economists such as Arakelian's *Upravlenie sotsialisticheskoi promyshlennosti* (*Management of Socialist Industry*) and on Party periodicals such as *Partiinaya Zhizn* (*Party Life*).

Available printed discussions were not found adequate for a survey of the difficulties produced in practice by the contradiction within the system of organization and for an examination of the methods used in resolving these difficulties. Much relevant information on this topic, as on the topic of the preceding section (see Appendix B, page 107) was found in the pages dedicated to "Party Life" in *Pravda*. However, to round out our knowledge we found it necessary to study some of the postwar Soviet novels based on industrial themes and to interview a number of DP engineers and technicians.

A full analysis of the organization and operation of industry in any society must include a number of analytically distinguishable factors. Purely economic and technological considerations, geographical and demographical factors are undoubtedly of foremost importance. That in this study the emphasis has been placed on psychocultural factors is owing in part to our own professional orientation and also to the very character of the premises upon which Soviet industrial organization is based.

Two basic differences between these premises and those which underly American theories and plans of industrial organization must be pointed out.

While American organizational blueprints are based on a consideration of the particular industrial complex to be erected, Soviet blueprints, as previously stated, are explicitly derived from a number of universal premises about the organization of human activity. While Americans tend to operate on the belief that the individual is only partially affected by the exercising of any particular role, Soviet theory emphasizes that the whole of human personality is involved in the successful performance of a job. Also, in American blueprints, considerations of morale or efficiency are usually relegated to the background. It is taken for granted that there exists a large labor force composed of individuals whose performance will not be greatly affected by the forms of organization in which they are placed. Changes in line or staff relationships are not expected to make a Dr. Jekyll out of a Mr. Hyde.

Grounds which are just as realistic can be found for the emphasis on morale in Soviet industrial organization. Soviet leaders and industry experts have attempted to harness to herculean industrial tasks a new and undisciplined labor force, relatively untrained in matters of timing and precision; the individuals who compose this labor force are believed to respond powerfully to the form of the organization in which they are placed. Psychological states are assumed to lend themselves to a high degree of manipulation, and performance is believed to be greatly and immediately affected by them.

The psychological premises underlying Soviet administrative theory and the structure of Soviet industrial organization have oscillated in the last decade or so between what can be considered as a complex of Great Russian attitudes regarding leadership and authority and a slowly emerging Soviet ideal of personality and social organization. While these traditional attitudes become increasingly predominant as one reaches down to the more concrete aspects of Soviet industrial reality, to the actual behavior—to the actual interaction among members of the industrial apparatus (particularly in spots geographically removed from centers of political authority, such as the Trans-Caucasus region)—they still permeate the most abstract theoretical discussions, resulting in insoluble contradictions even at this level.

The traditional Great Russian attitudes to which we have referred, attitudes tied to a long historical experience with arbitrary bureaucracy, are expressed in the concepts of *rukovodstvo* and *upravlenie*. The term *upravlenie*, which can be translated as "administration," or "direction," or "regulation," refers to those aspects of authority which are felt by Russians to be restrictive, all-embracing, impersonal, inanimate, and, consequently, arbitrary. While a careful examination of the nuances which differentiate the Russian concept from the American term *administration* is impossible in the present summary, we must point out the degree to which the Russian term is more encompassing than its American counterpart, a difference which reflects the Great Russian belief that it is *upravlenie* which in a sense gives the personality its form, and that without it the individual would act in explosive spurts of volatile energy.

The opposite pole of this Great Russian set of attitudes regarding leadership and authority emerges in the term *rukovodstvo* (literally, the act of leading by the hand), a concept which evokes a direct, positive, live relationship among individuals or among highly personalized collective concepts such as the Party and the masses, a relationship characterized by guidance and teaching and by the absence of compulsion. To this category of leadership are assigned the functions of planning and control. Only organs of *rukovodstvo* can issue the directives upon which planning for the future and organization of the present are based, since only they possess the insight and foresight necessary for the task. These organs alone, according to these traditional attitudes, can—by virtue of the psychological immediacy of their relationship to the masses—control and redress the abuses of bureaucracy, arouse in the masses the energy and enthusiasm required to break through bureaucracy's impersonal and arbitrary restrictions, and spur them on to the tasks ahead, whether a holy war against the foreign invader or the building of socialism.

The aged principles which we have outlined are still expected today to govern, to a large degree, the interaction of Party and non-Party organs of industrial leadership and administration and also partially to delineate within the intra-Party structure the relationship between the Party summit, its middle echelons—*oblast* (regional), city, and *raion* (district) committees—and the Party masses (primary Party organizations).

The adherence of Soviet leaders to this dogma, their assignment of *rukovodstvo* to Party organs and of the onus of *upravlenie* to non-Party organs in industry, of *rukovodstvo* to the summit and *upravlenie* to the middle echelons of the intra-Party structure, need not be explained purely by their belief in this body of doctrine. This division of functions provides a highly effective channel for diverting popular dissatisfaction from the Party leadership and an apparent remedy for the feared dissociation of the leadership from the masses which seems endemic in the Soviet elite. While the attitudes expressed in the concepts of *rukovodstvo* and *upravlenie* constitute today an important, if not always explicitly stressed, aspect of theory and practice in Soviet industrial organization, they have been slowly receding under the pressure of a new operative ideal of personality and social organization which has been emerging during the last two decades. For a highly articulated picture of the application of these still-surviving attitudes, it is useful to turn to the structure of organization of Soviet industry before 1934.

The onset of rapid industrialization in the Soviet Union was accompanied by a sharp increase in the need for specificity of timing and purpose in the efforts of the untrained labor force and administrative personnel upon whose shoulders this huge task lay. The administrative-regulative organs, the organs of *upravlenie* which were to supervise the fulfillment of the planned assignments and to provide the pressure needed for making individuals conform to the specific and delicate needs of highly geared and complex industrial giants, were organized at first in a characteristic fashion. Since the problem was conceived as one of molding individuals within the confines of organizational restraint, it was felt that the more precisely an organization defined and distinguished an individual's task, the more likely he was to fulfill his planned assignment. In accordance with this logic, the functional principle of organization was universally applied in all branches and at all levels of the operative organs of the Soviet industrial apparatus. This principle of organization was followed not only in regional Party committees and industrial trusts, but also in the smallest factory shops and in the Party cells of those shops. The universal application of this principle resulted in such absurdities as the division of a small shop administration of fewer than ten people into sectors of current production plans, cost norms, quality norms, supplies, labor organizations, and so on.

The structure of the administrative hierarchy also conformed in this period to the principle of *upravlenie*. Industrial ministries did not as yet exist, and the various branches of Soviet industry operated under the all-embracing supervision of the Supreme Economic Council. This tendency to set up catch-all administrative-regulative organs also appeared at lower levels of the administrative hierarchy in the predilection expressed for the *kombinat* forms of organization—large, unwieldy administrative structures which incorporated, sometimes with little logic, industrial units considered to be somehow related.

The organizational observance of the distinction between *rukovodstvo* and *upravlenie* was reflected by the rather rigid segregation, even within the non-Party structure, of planning and control functions from the function of administration. The political directives upon which planning is based were issued then, as they are today, by the Central Committee of the Party, and the spelling out and execution of those directives concerned purely with labor organizations were, then as now, a basic responsibility of Party organizations at various levels of the apparatus. A distinctive feature of this phase of the history of Soviet industrial organization, however, was the overwhelming concentration, the high degree of centralization, and the economic elaboration of these directives in the hands of the *Gosplan*, the State Planning Commission.

Control was organized in a similar fashion. Within the non-Party administrative structure this function was delegated to the Labor Peasant Inspection (RKI), a body which was expected continuously to control and check operations in every niche and nook of the Soviet economic apparatus and to correct the malfunctions discovered in this process of roving inspection. The control function of Party organizations over the administrative hierarchy and over the enterprises themselves was just as elastically defined.

The system of industrial organization which we have just outlined had evidenced, by the middle thirties, its complete unwieldiness and inefficiency. The functional organization of the administrative structure itself provided an ideal setting for what is called depersonalization in Soviet language, that is, escape from responsibility—passing the buck for failure. Further, excessive centralization and segregation of planning made frequent revisions of the plans, according to changes in the economic picture, almost impossible to achieve. Finally, the elastic definition of control and its concentration in the hands of external organs confronted these outside organs with the dilemma of either permitting the system to jam or of themselves taking over the current administration of the industrial apparatus. The pressure on the control organs, both Party and non-Party, to take over the current administation of the enterprises under their supervision was reinforced by a practice still current in Soviet administration: since the successful fulfillment of tasks was asserted to be dependent only on good organizational planning and efficient control (today, *verification* in Soviet language), the organs concerned with organizational planning and control were assigned complete responsibility for the successful fulfillment of tasks by the organizations under their supervision.

In the middle thirties, coincident with the maturation of a new generation of *Soviet Man*, a generation assumed to be endowed with more self-discipline, with a better sense of purpose and timing than its forebears, a new ideal of leadership and authority and a new definition of the organization of action were stressed by Soviet leaders. Within this new approach they began to remold the structure of industrial organization and, to a lesser extent, Soviet industrial practice.

The new ideal of leadership and authority, expressed in the concept of *edinonachalie* (literally, one-man leadership), stressed the necessity for a "full" concentration of both authority and responsibility for an organization in a single leader; it demanded "the incontrovertible subordination of the collective of workers to the single will of the leader." A measure of authority in both planning and control was entrusted to the heads of the administrative organs.

In line with these changes in the ideal of leadership, the definition of the organization of action underwent drastic verbal revision at the 1934 Party Congress. A closer union of planning, execution, and control was to be achieved, "a unity of word and action, of decision and fulfillment." Accordingly, the task of continuous roving inspection was assigned to the staff of the administrative structure and to the leaders of their subordinate enterprises, and the activities of external organs of control were to be limited to the verification of fulfillment of specific directives.

The new attitudes toward leadership and the organization of activity were to be reflected in the *productive territorial* organization of the industrial pyramid, and, indeed, they were observed in the overhauling of the structure of the *operational administrative organs.* According to the productive territorial principle, as we have seen, every production division, whether brigade, division, shop, enterprise, trust, chief administration, or ministry was to be headed by a leader with full authority and responsibility for the work of the division. The leader of the production division was to receive his assignments only from the leader of the production division at the next higher echelon and to be subordinate only to him. Functional organs, according to this ideal system of organization, were to be fully subordinated to the production leaders and were forbidden to give orders to lower echelons.

The reorganization of the administrative machinery according to the *productive territorial* principle and *edinonachalie* was calculated, in the eyes of Soviet leaders, to eliminate irresponsibility and to encourage individual initiative among the members of the administrative personnel. By the setting up of a direct and shortened line of responsibility down to the production level—a chain of authority, each link of which was entrusted to a single person—it was also designed to provide satisfactory contact between the top and the bottom of the pyramid, to realize in a more efficient manner the desired psychological immediacy between the leaders and the masses.

The new principles of organization were, on the whole, observed, if we consider the overhauled administrative structure alone. The Supreme Economic Council was subdivided into a number of production ministries. Most *kombinats* were dissolved and replaced by smaller, less unwieldy industrial units. Serious attempts were made to subordinate functional divisions to production organizations on the same hierarchical level from the ministries (commisariats) and their chief administrations (*upravlenie*) down to the plants and the shops. The function of current planning was to a large degree decentralized by placing a measure of responsibility for it in the hands of the planning divisions of the various hierarchical levels of the production ministries. The whole responsibility for inspection was turned over, on paper, to the heads of the enterprises themselves and to their direct superiors, and the Labor Peasant Inspection was accordingly replaced by Committees of Party and Soviet Control with much narrower functions. (In 1940 the Commission of Soviet Control became the Ministry of State Control, under the narrow jurisdiction of which comes the correction of criminal financial abuses.)

If one includes, as one must, the organs of Party leadership and control in this outline of Soviet industrial organization, the picture is drastically altered, even on a purely structural level. The 18th Party Congress of 1939, to be sure, abolished the industrial sections of the Party in order to strengthen the *edinonachalie*, the one-man leadership and control of management, and it severely forbade any usurpation by Party organizations of managerial functions. But the very same Congress reaffirmed the necessity for supervision by the Party organizations over the enterprises, both in organizational planning and control.

The formalistic character of the formulas by which the mutual relations of Party organs and industrial management are usually defined in newspaper editorial and conference resolutions allows easily for the many shifts on this question to which the Party Line has been subjected in the last decade. The type of injunction which encompassed all these shifts and gyrations would substantially state (in Soviet language) that "Party organizations should be the leaders of production, encourage technical initiative, be fully and continuously familiar with the work of the enterprises, and yet not get immersed in details, not take over managerial functions, not subject management to a petty tutelage." It is easy to see how any change of emphasis in this double-edged formula might constitute a major shift in the Party Line.

A review of the last decade of Soviet industrial administration gives some credence to the hypothesis that Soviet leaders have tended to regress most from the new *edinonachalie* ideal to the old formula of *rukovodstvo* and *upravlenie* in periods of acute political and economic stress.

In accordance with this hypothesis, the Party Line veered in 1941 to an emphasis on the active leadership of enterprises by Party organs, a shift which was reflected in the structure of organization by the effective restoration of the industrial divisions of the Party at the *oblast* (regional) and city levels, through the creation of industrial and transport secretariats. The outbreak of the war was accompanied by a frank concentration of power in Party organs, and, insofar as the supervision over factories was concerned, in the hands of the secretaries of the Party city and regional committees. The newspaper editorials during the war period were completely one-sided in their repeated calls for more vigorous leadership of industry by Party organizations.

With the end of the war emergency, the Party Line, as expressed in the Press, veered back, on the whole, to demands that Party organizations refrain from taking over managerial functions, but it shifted again at the end of 1947 and since then has been calling on Party members to take their economic responsibilities more seriously. (Our survey of the Soviet Press ends at the beginning of 1949.)

While the Party industrial organs provided a most glaring illustration of the way in which the principles of *edinonachalie* and of unity in current planning, execution, and verification of fulfillment are breached in the very structuring of Soviet industrial organization, they do by no means constitute the only instance of usurpation of managerial functions in administrative practice. Even administrative aides such as chief engineers or representatives of functional divisions, such as chief bookkeepers or *Gosplan* delegates engage in such interference throughout the administrative apparatus.

The causes for these violations of the rules are already to be found in the rules themselves, in the very legal statements which are supposed to uphold the new principles of organization. We find, for example, that the legal definition of the full authority (*polnoe vlast*) of the head of the enterprise is a relative concept, that it merely signifies that, of all the staff of the enterprise, he is given the most (*naibolshyi*) rights. We find that the administrative aides and the representatives of functional divisions who interfere with management are driven to do so because they are fully responsible legally for the state of the enterprise.

This wide assignment of responsibility, extending beyond the area of the individual's control, is partially responsible for another kind of breach of the territorial-productive principle of organization and of *edinonachalie*. The middle echelons of both the Party and the non-Party hierarchies, which are assigned total responsibility for the successful operation of subordinate administrative organs and enterprises, cannot afford to rely on unwieldy hierarchical channels. They are driven to act directly upon the administration of the enterprises, to reorganize their work and to check upon results achieved through the intermediary of their own plenipotentiaries. Yet, according to the accounts of DP's, the visits of commissions from Party and non-Party centers, from Party regional or city committees, or from chief industrial administrations usually result either in further jamming of the administrative system or in drastic changes in personnel which do not change very much the chaotic state of affairs. And if this interference results in serious disruption of output, Party regional or city committees, while they cannot now be asserted to be indifferent to their economic tasks, can always be accused of excessive interference with plant management or with the violation of the autonomy of Primary Party Organizations.

The managers, administrators, and Party representatives who are confronted with this degree of industrial disorganization and division of authority, and yet are expected to meet very high production quotas, tend to respond in either of two fashions: They may, particularly if their enterprises are located near political power centers, play the rules of the game and submit one another to inhuman pressures. Under this order of things, the chief administration makes the life of the manager miserable, the Party City Committee presses on the Party factory secretary, and the latter in turn threatens the factory manager. Alternatively, especially if the enterprises concerned are located in outlying regions, the people in authority may engage in "family relations." They may stand by one another in falsifying production figures, in attributing fictitious reasons to accidents and breakdowns, and for a certain period of time, as retribution is never far off, the Party secretary and the plant manager may be able to go horseback riding together every morning.

The structure of the Soviet apparatus provides an alternative channel by which officials may be able to reduce the intolerable pressures to which they are subjected. This system of organization is characterized by a high degree of duplication of and interference with authority up to the very top of the power hierarchy. We have already alluded to the overlapping of authority and to the violation of hierarchical lines which characterize the functioning of the Party pyramid and the apparatus of industrial ministries. We have also referred to the overlapping of authority and to the duplications of functions in the relations between these structures. The interference of yet a third organization, the MVD (Ministry of Internal Affairs), confuses areas of authority even further. To the MVD is assigned the general responsibility of safeguarding industry from enemies of the regime. In view of the very elastic and wide definition given to sabotage in Soviet culture, a phenomenon undoubtedly related to the general emphasis on will and control in the personality, the officials of the MVD, like members of other hierarchies, are in fact assigned responsibilities which extend far beyond the formal definition of their roles.

The response to this situation made by higher officials is a struggle for power, for possession of power signifies less vulnerability and greater control over situations for which responsibility is unlimited. This power is found through personal alignments, informal cliques, which gratify both higher officials' need for greater informal authority and subordinates' desire for protection from pressure by superiors.

In the preceding discussion we have attempted to show that the present system of Soviet industrial organization is an amalgam of old and new patterns of organization, which themselves reflect traditional Great Russian and new Soviet attitudes about leadership, authority, and the organization of action. We have pointed out how the combination of internal and external controls, which has resulted from this mixture, tends to contribute to the continuous jamming of the industrial system. Since this is the case, one may well ask for the reasons why the system functions as well as it does.

The positive and compensatory feature of the system of organization we have described resides, we believe, in the mobilization by Party organizations of the workers' energies and initiative through such devices as production conferences, collective agreements, and socialist competition. We can only briefly summarize

SOVIET ATTITUDES TOWARD AUTHORITY

here some of the major characteristics of these organized forms of collective action and of the discussions, led by Party agitators and propagandists, which usually precede them.[163]

In factory meetings, Party propagandists and agitators may encourage criticism of the management by the workers and attempt to foster the feeling that the Party is a benevolent authority which sides with them against the frequently treacherous *intelligentsia* (the managerial staff) of the factory. The workers are expected to draw the conclusion that, through their own efforts and under the guidance (*rukovodstvo*) of the Party, they can overcome the passivity or resistance of organs of *upravlenie* and break through lines of administrative restraint. The organization of collective agreements and of socialist competition is similarly calculated to arouse in the workers a belief in their own importance and in the close affective bond which ties them to the Party.

Party activities are conducted in this connection according to extremely fluid organizational lines. The meetings which lay the groundwork for the socialist competition include participants from various levels of the administrative hierarchy of the plant, and in this way lines of organizational restraint are again effectively bridged.

Party leadership of workers' collectives in factories undoubtedly contributes to the disorganization of factory administrations. Its encouragement of distrust of the managerial staff by the workers undoubtedly encourages conflicts and breaches of discipline by the labor force. But these negative features are more than counterbalanced by the mobilization of initiative and enthusiasm achieved by these Party activities.

Sources used by L. H. Haimson in Summary of Conclusions of Research on Party and Non-Party Organizations in Soviet Industry.

For studies of problems of Party organization:

Abranov, A., and Aleksandrov, *The Party in the Period of Reconstruction* (*Partiya v rekonstruktsionnyi period*), Moscow, 1934.
Bakhshiyev, *Organizational Foundations of the Bolshevik Party* (*Organizatsionnye osnovy bolshevistskoi partii*), Moscow, 1943.
Bubnov, Andrei, *All-Union Communist Party* (*of Bolsheviks*) (*VKP(b)*), Moscow, 1938.
Stalin, *Collected Works* (*Sochinenia*).
———, *Leninism,* London, 1932.
———, "Mastering Bolshevism," *Bol'shevik,* April 1, 1937.
Yaroslavskii, E., *History of the CPSU* (*b*), (*Istoriya VKP(b)*), Moscow, 1926.
———, *How Lenin Dealt with the Party Purge* (*Kak Lenin otnosilsya k chistke partii*), Moscow, 1929.
———, *Verification and Purging of the Party Ranks,* Moscow, 1933.
17th Congress of the All-Union Communist Party (*XVII s'ezd Vsesoyuznoi Kommunisticheskoi Partii*), stenographic account, Moscow, 1934.

---

[163] See Appendix F.

18th Congress of the All-Union Communist Party (*XVIII s'ezd Vsesoyuznoi Kommunisticheskoi Partii*), stenographic account, Moscow, 1939.
1938 Plenum of the Central Committee of the All-Union Communist Party, Resolution, *Partiinoye Stroitelstvo (Party Construction)*, February, 1938.

For studies of Soviet industrial organization and Party leadership in industry:

PERIODICALS

Partiinoye Stroitelstvo (Party Construction), 1939–40.
Partiinaya Zhizn (Party Life), 1945–49.
Bol'shevik, 1940–49.
Novyi Mir (New World), 1944–49.
Oktyabr' (October), 1944.
Znamya (Banner), 1944–47.
Sovetskoye Gosudarstvo i Pravo (Soviet Government and Law) (scattered issues).
Promyshlennost' (Industry) (scattered issues).

NEWSPAPERS

Pravda, 1944–49.

BOOKS

Arakelian, E., *Management of Socialist Industry (Upravlenie sotsialisticheskoi promyshlennosti)*, Moscow, 1947.
Baykov, A., *The Development of the Soviet Economic System*, Cambridge University Press, London, 1946.
Bienstock, G., S. Schwarz, and A. Yugow, *Management in Russian Industry and Agriculture*, Oxford University Press, New York, 1944.
Chernyak, N., *Party Organization and Socialist Competition (Partiinaya organizatsiya i sotsialisticheskoe sorevnovanie)*, Moscow, 1947.
Dewar, M., *The Organization of Soviet Industry*, mimeographed study, Royal Institute of International Affairs, London, 1945.
Evtikhiev, I. I., and V. A. Vlasov, *Administrative Law (Administrativnoe pravo)*, Moscow, 1946.
Littlepage, J., and D. Best, *In Search of Soviet Gold*, Harcourt, Brace and Company, Inc., New York, 1938.
Panova, V., *Kruzhilikha*, Moscow, 1945.
Scott, J., *Behind the Urals*, Houghton Mifflin Company, New York, 1942.
Towster, J., *Political Power in the U.S.S.R.*, Oxford University Press, 1948.
18th Conference of the All-Union Communist Party (*XVIII Konferentsia Vsesoyuznoi Kommunisticheskoi Partii*), Moscow, February, 1941.

APPENDIX D

SOURCE MATERIALS USED BY OTHER MEMBERS OF THE RESEARCH GROUP

Sources used by Nathan Leites.

The Crime of the Zinoviev Opposition, The Assassination of Sergei Mironovich Kirov, Cooperative Publishing Society of Foreign Workers in the USSR, Moscow, 1935.

Report of Court Proceedings in the Case of the Trotskyite-Zinovievite Terrorist Centre, heard before the Military Collegium of the Supreme Court of the USSR, Moscow, August 19–24, 1936, published by the People's Commissariat of Justice of the USSR, Moscow, 1936.

Report of Court Proceedings in the Case of the Anti-Trotskyite Centre, Moscow, January 23–30, 1937.

Report of Court Proceedings in the Case of the Anti-Soviet "Bloc of Rights and Trotskyites," Moscow, March 2–13, 1938.

The Case of Leon Trotsky, report of hearings on the charges made against him in the Moscow trials by the Preliminary Commission of Inquiry, Harper & Brothers, New York, 1937.

Ciliga, Anton, *The Russian Enigma,* The Labour Book Service, London, no year.

Fischer, Ruth, *Stalin and German Communism,* Harvard University Press, Cambridge, Mass., 1948.

Gorer, Geoffrey, and John Rickman, *The People of Great Russia: A Psychological Study,* Cresset Press, London, 1949.

Koestler, Arthur, *Darkness at Noon,* The Modern Library, New York, no year.

Krivitsky, W. G., *In Stalin's Secret Service,* Harper & Brothers, New York, 1939.

Letter of an Old Bolshevik, Rand School Press, New York, 1937.

Life of the Archpriest Avvakum by Himself, in *A Treasury of Russian Spirituality,* G. P. Fedotov (comp. and ed.), Sheed & Ward, Inc., New York, 1948.

Not Guilty, report of the Commission of Inquiry into the charges made against Leon Trotsky in the Moscow trials, Harper & Brothers, New York, 1938.

Plisnier, Charles, *Faux passeports,* Editions R. A. Correa, Paris, 1937 (trans. by Nathan Leites and Elsa Bernaut).

Schachtman, Max, *Behind the Moscow Trial,* Pioneer Publishers, New York, 1936.

Slater, Humphrey, *Conspirator,* Harcourt, Brace and Company, Inc., New York, 1948.

Souvarine, Boris, *Stalin,* Longmans, Green & Co., Inc., New York, 1939.

The Soviet-Yugoslav Dispute, Royal Institute of International Affairs, London, 1948.

Ypsilon, *Pattern for World Revolution,* Ziff-Davis Publishing Company, New York, 1947.

Sources used by Elsa Bernaut.

Bubnov, A., *Basic Moments in the Development of the Communist Party* (*Osnovnye momenty razvitiya kommunisticheskoi partii*), Moscow, 1923.

Bukharin, N., *The Economics of the Transition Period* (*Ekonomika perekhodnovo perioda*), Moscow, 1920 (also various articles in periodicals and papers quoted below).

Lenin, V. I., *Collected Works* (*Polnoye sobraniye*).
Preobrazhenski, E., *From the NEP to Socialism* (*Ot nepa k sotsialisma*), Moscow, 1922.
Stalin, J., *Leninism or Trotskyism* (*Leninism ili Trotskyism*), Moscow, 1924.
————, *On the Right Deviation of the CPSU* (*O pravom uklone v VKP*), 1929.
Trotsky, L., *History of the Russian Revolution* (*Istoria Russkoi Revolyutsii*), Berlin, 1931–33.
————, *My Life* (*Moya Zhizn*), Berlin, 1930.
————, *Bulletin of the Opposition* (*Byulleten' Oppozitsii*), Paris.
Zorin, V., *On the Right Danger to the Communist Party* (*O pravoi opasnostii VKP(B)*).
The Communist Internationale in Documents (*Kommunisticheskii Internatsional v dokumentakh*).
Record of the Party Congresses.
Record of the Party Plenums.
Kommunist (periodical).
Partiinoye Stroitelstvo (*Party Construction*) (periodical).
Bol'shevik (periodical).
Partiinaya Zhizn (*Party Life*) (periodical).
Pravda (daily).
Izvestia (daily).

German

Rote Fahne, Berlin (daily).
Imprecor (periodical).
Fahne des Kommunismus (periodical).

Russian (additional)

Report of the Court Proceedings in the Case of the Trotskyite-Zinovievite Terrorist Centre, Moscow, 1936.
Report of the Court Proceedings in the Case of the Anti-Soviet Trotskyite Centre, Moscow, 1937.
Report of the Court Proceedings in the Case of the Anti-Soviet "Rights and Trotskyites," Moscow, 1938.

French

Souvarine, B., *Staline,* Paris, 1935.
Ciliga, A., *Au Pays du Grand Mensonge,* Paris, 1938.
Rossi, A., *Physiologie du Parti Communiste Francais,* Paris, 1948.
Yaroslawski, E., *Histoire du Parti Communiste de l'URSS,* Paris, 1931.
L'Humanité (daily).

English

Not Guilty, Report of the Commission of Inquiry into the Charges against Leon Trotsky, Harper & Brothers, New York, 1938.
Krivitsky, W. G., *In Stalin's Secret Service,* Harper & Brothers, New York, 1939.
Mosely, P., "The Moscow Trials," *Yale Review,* 1938.
Shachtman, M., *Behind the Moscow Trials,* New York, 1936.
Report of the Royal Commission, Appointed under Order in Council P.C. 411 of February 5, 1946, to investigate the facts relating to and the circumstances surrounding the communication, by public officials and other persons in positions of trust, of secret and confidential information to agents of a foreign power, Ottawa, June 27, 1946.

Sources used by Nelly S. Hoyt.

For Studies of Komsomol:

Komsomolskaya Pravda, 1945–48.

Molodoi Bol'shevik, all issues for 1947.

Shokhin, A., *Short Sketch of the History of the Komsomol (Kratkii ocherk istorii Komsomola),* Molodaia Gvardia, Moscow, 1926.

Andreyev, A., *Communist Education of Youth and the Tasks of the Komsomol (O Kommunisticheskom vospitanii molodezhi),* Molodaia Gvardia, Moscow, 1938.

What Was Decided at the Tenth All-Union Congress of the VLKSM (Chto ryeshil desiatovo vsesoyuznovo s'ezda), Molodaia Gvardia, Moscow, 1936.

The New Constitution of the VLKSM (Ustav V sesoiuznovo Leninskovo Kommunisticheskii Soiuz Molodezhi), Molodaia Gvardia, Moscow, 1940.

Victorov, R., *Ilyitch and the Komsomol (Ilich i Komsomol),* Molodaia Gvardia, Moscow, 1928.

Stalin, J., *About the Komsomol (O Komsomole),* Molodaia Gvardia, Moscow, 1936.

Mishakova, O., *Stalin's Constitution and Soviet Youth (Stalinskaia Konstitutsia i Sovetskaia molodezh),* Molodaia Gvardia, Moscow, 1945.

For Studies of the Satire:

Zoshchenko, M., collected works.

For Studies of the Folklore:

Andreyev, N., *Russian Folklore (Russkii Folklor),* Anthology for Higher Pedagogical Institutions, 1938.

Byliny, introduction by E. A. Latsko, St. Petersburg, 1911.

Bylini of the North (Byliny severa), Vol. 1, Mekhen and Pechora, introduction and commentaries by A. Astakhova, Leningrad, 1938.

Kriukovoi, M. S., *Bylini,* Vols. 1 and 2, Moscow, 1941.

Chuvash Tales (Chuvashskiye skazki), Moscow, 1937.

Tales of the Altai Masters (Legendy i byli), 1938.

Lenin, Stalin, *Creations of the Peoples of the USSR,* Moscow, 1938.

Lenin and Stalin in the Poetry of the Peoples of the USSR (Lenin i Stalin v poezii narodov SSSR), Moscow, 1938.

Kriukova, M. S., *Legends about Lenin (Skazanie o Lenine),* Moscow, 1938.

Klimovich, L. I. (ed.), *Anthology of the Literature of the Peoples of the USSR (Khrestomatiya po literature narodov SSSR),* Moscow, 1947.

Miller, Orest, *Ilya Muromets and the Kievan Heroes (Ilya Muromets i boga tyrstvo Kievskoye),* St. Petersburg, 1870.

Russian Popular Epos (Russkii narodnyi epos), Comparative Texts, Moscow, 1947.

Azadovskii (ed.), *Russian Folklore (Russkii folklor)* (volume on epic poetry), 1935.

Shelly, G. K., *Folktales of the Peoples of the Soviet Union,* London, 1945.

Soviet Folklore (Sovietskii folklor), collection of articles, Leningrad, 1939.

Sovietskii Folklor (periodical).

Jakobson, R., Commentary to A. N. Afanasev, *Russian Fairy Tales,* New York, 1945.

Azadovskii, M., *New Folklore (Novyi Folklor).*

Byalik, B., *Gorky and the Science of Folklore (Gorkii i nauka o folklor).*

Dymshits, A., *Lenin and Stalin in the Folklore of the Peoples of the USSR (Lenin i Stalin v folklor narodov SSSR).*

Astakhova, A., *The Russian Hero Epos and Contemporary Bylini (Russkii geroicheskii epos i sovremenniye byliny).*

Vladmirskii, G., *The Singers of the Stalin Epoch* (*Pevtsy Stalinskoi epokhy*).
Abramkin, V., *The Folklore of the Civil War* (*Folklor grazhdanskoi voiny*).
Kaletskii, P., *The New Tale* (*Novaya skazka*).
Eventov, I., *The Soviet Song* (*Sovietskaya pesnya*).

Sources used by Vera Schwarz.

Literaturnaya Entsiklopediya (*Literary Encyclopedia*), published in Moscow (11 volumes).
Bol'shaya Sovetskaya Entsiklopediya (*The Great Soviet Encyclopedia*).
Malaya Sovetskaya Entsiklopediya (*The Little Soviet Encyclopedia*).
History of Russian Children's Literature (*Istoriya Russkoi detskoi literatury*), published by the Scientific Pedagogical Publishing House of the Ministry of Education, Moscow, 1948.
Yarmolinsky, Avram (ed.), *A Treasury of Russian Verse,* The Macmillan Company, New York, 1949.
Novyi Mir (*The New World*), organ of the Union of Soviet Writers, a monthly published in Moscow by the publishing house *Izvestia.*
Oktyabr' (*October*), organ of the Union of Soviet Writers, a monthly published in Moscow by the publishing house *Pravda.*
Krasnaya Nov' (*The Red Virgin Soil*), organ of the Union of Soviet Writers, published in Moscow, suspended in 1941.
Znamya (*The Standard*), organ of the Union of Soviet Writers, a monthly published in Moscow since the beginning of the thirties by the publishing house *Sovietski Pisatel'* (*The Soviet Writer*).
Zvezda (*The Star*), organ of the Union of Soviet Writers, a monthly published in Leningrad by the Unified State Publishing House.
Ogonyok (*The Light*), published by the publishing house *Pravda.*
Leningrad Almanac, published in Leningrad by the Newspaper, Magazine and Book Publishing House.
Almanac Sever (*The North*), published in Arkhangelsk by the Unified State Publishing House.
Sibirskiye Ogni (*Siberian Lights*), published in Novosibirsk.
Literaturnyi Kritic (*The Literary Critic*), suspended in December, 1940.
Literaturnaya Gazeta (*The Literary Newspaper*), organ of the Board of the Union of Soviet Writers published since 1947 twice a week, Moscow.
Sovetskoye Iskusstvo (*Soviet Art*), organ of the Department of Movie Art of the Committee dealing with Arts of the Council of the Ministers of the USSR and of the Committee of the Council dealing with the Architecture of the USSR, a weekly, Moscow.
Kultura i Zhizn' (*Culture and Life*), newspaper of the propaganda division of the Central Committee of the Communist Party, published weekly in Moscow since 1946.
Bol'shevik (*Bolshevik*), theoretical and political magazine of the Central Committee of the Communist Party, Moscow.
Pravda, organ of the Central Committee of the Communist Party, a daily newspaper.
Izvestia, a daily newspaper published in Moscow.
Sotsialisticheskoye Zemledeliye (*Socialist Agriculture*), a daily, Moscow.
Trud (*Labor*), organ of the All-Union Central Council of Trade Unions, published in Moscow.
Voprosy Istorii (*Problems of History*), issued by the publishing house *Pravda,* Moscow.
Pedagogika (*Pedagogy*), Moscow, 1948.

Sources used by Ralph T. Fisher, Jr.

Aleksandrov, G., *et al.* (ed.), *Political Dictionary* (*Politicheskii Slovar'*), 1940, pp. 90–92.

"Eleventh Congress of the Young Communist League of the Soviet Union," *Current Digest of the Soviet Press,* I:13 (April 26, 1949), pp. 13–22; and I:14 (May 3, 1949), pp. 8–22.

Fischer, Louis, *Thirteen Who Fled,* Harper & Brothers, New York, 1949.

Kaftanov, S., "The Komsomol in the Struggle to Master Advanced Science and Technique" ("Komsomol v bor'be za ovladeniye peredovoi naukoi i tekhnikoi"), *Izvestia,* March 29, 1949. *Komsomol' skaya Pravda,* March 29–31 and April 1–20, 1949.

Krivtsov, A. A., "Report of the Central Auditing Commission" ("Otchet tsentral'noi revizionnoi komissii"), *Komsomol' skaya Pravda,* March 31, 1949, pp. 3–4.

Mikhailov, N. A., "Report of the Central Committee of the VLKSM at the 11th Congress" ("Otchet TsK VLKSM XI s'ezdu"), *Komsomol' skaya Pravda,* March 30, 1949, pp. 2–3; March 31, 1949, pp. 2–3.

Shelepin, A. N., "Report of the Mandate Commission of the 11th Congress of the VLKSM" ("Doklad mandatnoi komissii XI s'ezda VLKSM"), *Komsomol' skaya Pravda,* April 1, 1949, p. 2.

Tyurin, N., "All-Union Leninist Communist League of Youth" in the *Great Soviet Encyclopedia (Bol'shaya Sovetskaia Entsiklopediya),* supplementary volume entitled *Soyuz Sovetskikh Sotsialisticheskikh Respublik* (USSR), 1948, pp. 1712–40.

EXCERPT CONCERNING THE COMMUNIST "ELECTION OF MAY, 1948, IN CZECHOSLOVAKIA"—TAKEN FROM CHAPTER XVI OF UNPUBLISHED MANUSCRIPT "CZECHS, SLOVAKS, AND COMMUNISM"

BY DAVID RODNICK

The Czech Communists worked on the assumption that "talking makes things so." In order to build up the "legality" of a one-party election, a campaign was begun on April 7, 1948, to make it appear that it was the "people" who wanted a unified election list; that the Communists preferred to take their chances in competition with the other "paper" political parties but it was up to the "people" to decide whether the government should have a one-party slate or separate party lists. The Communist leadership knew that in any free and open election, the Communist vote would have been an extremely small one. No one thing that the Communists had done since their assumption of complete power in February antagonized the non-Communist Czechs and even many within the Party as much as the hypocritical building-up of an artificial public opinion that was created for the Party to manipulate as puppets. Nothing showed the megalomania of the Communist Party leadership more than this tendency to project its desires onto paper organizations and a synthetic public opinion—a move which assumed a lack of critical intelligence on the part of the non-Communists. It was a striking example of the amorality of the Communists who cynically assumed that by throwing words to the people, the latter would accept them as realities. The level of rationalization which this political campaign employed was one that could have appealed only to psychotic individuals. The only possible motivation was that the Communists had the power, expected to keep it, but wanted to cloak their intention with a synthetic "legality" which they assumed would satisfy the Czechs. Only the Nazis could have equalled the contempt for the dignity and commonsense of the human being that the Communists displayed in their crude maneuvering. At the same time, they assumed a naïveté on the part of the outside world which would be willing to accept such an obvious hoax. Actually the Communists had gone the Nazis one better in preparing their unity list.

131

The maneuver started on April 7th when Antonin Zapotocky, who at that time was Deputy Prime Minister and Chairman of the Trades Union Council, addressed a meeting of this Council on how it should work in the coming election. In the course of his remarks, he said, "There is one more matter facing us in this question of the elections. This question must be discussed. It is a political question, for the results will determine the structure of the future Parliament. If the political parties of the regenerated National Front go independently into the election, what should our attitude be. Should we recommend separate lists of candidates of all individual parties, or *should we use the weight of our influence to see that the results of the election would be such as to give us a guarantee that future progress will be on the lines we want?* . . . [italics ours]

"I make this question a subject of discussion. We should frankly put the question to ourselves whether it is necessary for each party in our re-born National Front to present its own list of candidates or whether the time has already come to consider a joint election list."

Immediately according to plan, Evuzen Erban, the Minister of Social Welfare, General Secretary of the Trades Union Council and a prominent Social Democratic leader, rose to give his approval of Zapotocky's proposal to have a single election list. He said, "I am convinced that this proposal will meet with a great reception among the working class of our country, and that also all of our political leaders if they feel any responsibility to the nation and to the working class will wholeheartedly agree with this proposal. We shall thus succeed in creating the same harmony in both our economic and political life." Mr. Erban went on to make remarks which would seem to indicate that he felt guilty and on the defensive. In them, he appeared to work on the assumption that the single list, though it had been suggested for the first time only a few minutes before, was an accomplished fact. He went on to say, "In the West, they will of course lament that the disintegration of our democracy is continuing. Yes, the disintegration of our bourgeois democracy is continuing. We have no need to wage any political class warfare because we have won our battle. . . . The Western democracies and the capitalists of the West will naturally fail to understand us, and we won't even attempt to make them understand. We have our truth and they have theirs."[164]

After "deliberation," the Trades Union Council the next day passed unanimously a resolution calling upon "all political parties as well as the Central Action Committee of the National Front to negotiate the safe-guarding of the splendid victory over reaction by a joint election action."

On the same day, a spokesman for the Action Committee of the Communist-controlled Czech Socialist Party (before February, the National Socialist Party)

---

[164] *Daily Review*, Prague, April 8, 1948.

announced his "full support for a joint list." He declared he considered it his duty to convince all members of the Action Committee of his Party to support this "patriotic proposal." Then, on the same day, the Social Democratic Parliamentary group met and agreed to "recommend that the Presidium of the Party accept this proposal."[165] On the following day, the People's Party decided that "after considering all circumstances, we have decided to take a positive attitude toward the simplification of the election and to express our approval of the joint election list of the National Front.

"A joint list of candidates will prevent the traditional discord and strife of election campaigns. Now that there will be no election battle, the people can devote themselves calmly to their work. Many hours wasted at meetings will be saved, as well as much paper wasted on election posters."[166]

On the same day, the Press Section of the Central Action Committee of Czechoslovakia (completely composed of Communists, such as Gustav Barevs, one of the leading spokesmen for the Cominform in Czechoslovakia; J. Sila, the editor of the trade-union and Communist newspaper *Prace;* Vaclav Dolejsi, chairman of the Union of Czech Journalists, a Communist organization; Jiri Hronek, chief editor of the Czechoslovakian radio which has been in Communist hands since 1945 and Secretary-General of the International Organization of Journalists; along with the chiefs of divisions in the Ministry of Information, and the editors of the official Communist publication *Rude Pravo*) issued a statement in support of the joint election list. "Acceptance of this proposal," the statement said, "will prevent forever the *partisan misuse of the Press* and will enable the Press to devote itself *fully to creative criticism.*"[167] [italics ours]

The confusion even in propaganda tended to "let the cat out of the bag" when an editor in *Pravo Lidu,* the Communist-controlled Social Democratic paper, wrote on April 10th in support of this proposal, "The Social Democratic Party has no reason to oppose the joint election list proposal which is to express clearly and uncompromisingly the will of the Czechoslovak people to put an end to the bourgeois democratic political game and to enter a new path of unity of all people of good will. The Social Democratic Party agrees with Mr. Zapotocky's proposal without any ulterior motive. . . . It was the leftwing Social Democrats who helped to fight for the victory of the working class. It was the Social Democratic Party which foiled the plan of reaction to break up the majority of the government in Parliament. We shall never fear sincere cooperation with Communists and we therefore need not regard the joint election list with them as a way of *escaping* the wrath of the electorate."[168] [italics ours]

[165] *Ibid.,* April 9, 1948.
[166] *Ibid.,* April 10, 1948 (taken from *Lidova Demokracie,* same date).
[167] *Ibid.*
[168] *Ibid.*

As a result of this "persuasion" on the part of the "people," the Central Executive Committee of the Czechoslovakian Communist Party very reluctantly on April 10th decided to bow to the will of the synthetic public opinion which it had created and had tried to cloak with reality, and by an "unanimous vote" decided to go along with the other "people's representatives" to accept and approve the proposal for a joint election list. When we remarked to a fanatic Communist on April 11th how rapidly the proposal was made and then accepted by "public opinion," he enthusiastically replied, "Communism builds unity among the people and is therefore more efficient than the capitalistic bourgeois democracies."

Two days later, non-Communist Czechs were rather amused when the date of the coming "election" was changed from May 23rd to May 30th. The reason for this shift was given by the Communist press as being due to the fact that the earlier date would conflict with the opening of the All-Slav Agricultural Exhibition to be held in Prague on May 23rd. The election was considered "in the bag."

We have given this background to the election in some detail because we think it an excellent example of how the Communists even when in power still behave as conspirators. They make no attempts to be honest in their intentions with the people whom they are governing. They apparently feel it necessary to cloak their secret intentions with words which have no relationship to what they expect to do and which they utilize as substitutes for reality. The Communist leadership does not trust its own membership, and words are used only as a sop to build up some kind of a link with those they do not trust. Words to the Communists have no meaning except as a bridge to the non-Communist population in order to divert it from the intentions which the Communists think they are keeping secret. A good Communist pays little attention to these words. He is imbued with a faith that whatever the Party does is right and is done in order to build up Party power.

The use of words to translate unsavory intentions into socially-acceptable ones was well exemplified in the following article which appeared in the official Communist newspaper *Rude Pravo* on April 11th. "The Communist Party had been seriously preparing for an election campaign in competition with the other political parties. The Communists were looking forward to the election day when they could have shown the greatness of their Party in its full glory, and the fact that there is to be a joint election list does not mean that the Communist Party will play a less prominent role. The unanimous decision of the Party Executive Committee clearly reflects the responsible manner in which the Communists solve their statesmanlike tasks and the way in which they understand their leading position in the nation."[169]

---

[169] This sacrifice which the Communist Party was making was accepted because the other "paper" political parties which they controlled "insisted" upon cooperating with the Communists for the general welfare of the Communist Party.

An "opposition" was also permitted to put out its own list of candidates. But then came the veiled threat which was expressed in *Rude Pravo* on April 11th by a Communist spokesman who said, "If anyone opposes the People's Democracy, let him do so openly." If any group in the population wanted to present an opposition list of candidates at the election, it had to gather 1000 signatures on a petition which was to be turned over to the election committee of the People's Democracy (Communist Party) in order to make certain that none of these individuals were "enemies and saboteurs who were against the progress of the working class."

Some weeks before the so-called "election," every storekeeper was required to put in his front window a poster urging support for the unity list. In all public offices and railroad stations there were banners or placards with the words, "He who loves the Republic will vote for the Republic," or "White ticket—black thoughts," and so on. It took courage for an individual to use the white voting slip in the "election" on May 30th. In almost all polling stations, the box for the white ballots was out in the open and surrounded by watchers from the local Communist Party. Each voter had been given two ballots beforehand; a red ballot which had the government list inside and a white one which was blank. Each ballot was in an envelope and could be marked at home, sealed, and brought back to the voting station. There a voter's name was checked off the list and he was permitted to go to the back of the room where the ballot boxes were theoretically supposed to be behind screens. No screens were in any of the polling stations we heard of; both boxes were out in the open. The voter was supposed to drop a ballot in either the government box or the white-ballot box and to discard the ballot he did not use in either the wastebasket for the red ballots or the one for the white ballots. As many "paper" Communist watchers told us later on, it was very difficult to get by them. They were supposed to mark down the names of all individuals who voted the white ballot and to try to intimidate them by asking them if they weren't going in the wrong direction when they approached the white-ballot box. It was impossible to cast a ballot without everyone's knowing how one voted. Many individuals who wished to cast a white ballot, but were afraid of the consequences, used their red envelope, but instead of putting in the red ballot they inserted pictures of Thomas G. Masaryk, President Benes, Jan Masaryk, Franklin D. Roosevelt, Winston Churchill, caricatures of Josef Stalin, Gottwald, Hitler, toilet paper, or nothing. Many also wrote notes attacking the Communists. Official counters from various parts of Czechoslovakia told us later on that the Ministry of Interior in Prague confiscated ballot boxes without permitting them to be counted, or if they had already been counted, gave out abnormally low figures. One counter in a city of 35,000 told us that in his district alone he counted 860 white ballots, and friends of his who had also served as counters in other parts of the city told him afterward that they counted as much and sometimes more than in his district. The official count for white ballots in the whole city was 216! In other parts of Czechoslovakia we were told of similar instances, where the total white ballots for a whole town or city would be given out as much smaller than had been counted in only one district.

On the basis of the official figures put out by the Communists themselves on June 6th, 6.5 per cent of the voters abstained from voting, 3 per cent cast invalid votes, while 10.8 per cent cast white ballots. According to these statistics, a little over 20 per cent did not vote for the unity list. On the other hand, the Communists counted only what they considered the valid votes and to their great surprise discovered that they had 89.2 per cent of them! It was rather interesting that the largest numbers of white ballots counted by the government were in the industrial cities such as Zlin, Pardubice, Moravska-Ostrava, and Plzen where the official count showed between 16 and 20 per cent of white ballots. In the Catholic areas of Slovakia and Moravia, few white ballots were cast and the government received almost 100 per cent of the vote. In the Hana area of Moravia, however, the white ballots went up to 30 per cent. It was no fault of the Communists that they did not get 100 per cent throughout Czechoslovakia. Their failure to do so was mainly due to the large number of "Communist" watchers and counters who had no enthusiasm for interfering with the voters and who tried to make an accurate count of whatever white ballots were cast before they went to the Ministry of Interior. The latter put them through their special Communist tabulating machine which was geared to make certain that the final figure would be within certain limits. In later conversations with convinced Communists, we were told, "Well, maybe we didn't get 89 per cent, but we got at least 60 per cent." Most Czechs were quite surprised at the election result, because they had expected the Communists to get at least 99 per cent of the vote.

APPENDIX F

"TO AID THE AGITATOR,"
FROM *PRAVDA*, MAY 27, 1948

What follows is a translated quotation from a fairly complete report of an agitation meeting, conducted by one of the best agitators of the Stalingrad region, in a shop of the "Red October" metallurgical factory, an account published fully in *Pravda* for the benefit of other party agitators. To prepare for his discussion, the editor's preamble to this account states, the agitator, Andrei Koliada, studied a number of specified works by Lenin and Stalin and also used materials from newspapers. The foreman of the shop presented the agitator with facts about production, examples in particular brigades. Wall newspapers and diagrams about the growth of production in the shop and about the role of each brigade in the struggle for plan fulfillment were prepared in advance.

At the beginning of his talk, Comrade Koliada described the tasks laid by Stalin of overfulfilling prewar production in the first postwar Five-Year Plan. . . . He presents figures which illustrate the prewar industrial growth. . . . "You remember Comrades, what our factory was like in 1928. Here are sitting a number of older workers, they remember this very well. Maybe one of them will describe what the factory was like before the Five-Year plans. Let the young workers listen.

Kazenkov (a welder): I can tell. [He then described the technical backwardness of the factory in 1928.] Only after the reconstruction of the basic shops and the construction of new Martin furnaces did "Red October" become transformed into a first class metallurgical plant.

Koliada: Correctly said, Ivan Ivanovich.

[Koliada then describes the war destruction of the factory, which for anyone but Bolsheviks would have made the task of restoration appear impossible. He then tells of the postwar reconstruction.]

In the last thirty years, even Soviet people have changed. As Zhdanov said, "We are not today what we were yesterday, and will not be tomorrow what we are today. . . ." Some people may ask, "Why hasten the tempo and fulfill the Five-Year Plan in four years?" Maybe someone still thinks: Why hurry; it is better to fulfill the indicated plan and not realize its overfulfillment? Is that so?

Kurtin (another worker): No. To fulfill the plan in four years means to speed up the strengthening of our country, the beautifying of our lives.

Ivanov (another worker): Right, Comrade Kurtin, every one of us wants to improve his life, to have a good apartment, good food, good clothes, that our

137

children grow healthy and happy, that they study. Everyone of us wants that not only our children, but that we ourselves live in a Communist society. We fully deserve this because who if not we carried on our shoulders all the difficulties of this gigantic struggle . . . that we must work, work hard, to realize these goals.

Koliada: I fully agree with your ·words. The Party and Government are doing everything to improve the life of the workers, the peasants, and the intelligentsia. [As proof of this he cites the abolition of rationing, and the monetary reform.] Where in the capitalist world, could you find a state which has reconstructed its economy as rapidly after a severe war. [He speaks of inflation, unemployment in the United States.] And American workers have still worse days ahead. A crisis of terrific impact. A Five-Year Plan in four years is needed further because of the surviving agitation for war in foreign countries.

[Koliada now turns to the need for reducing costs. He criticizes a number of members of the managerial staff for their lack of concern over machinery. He then turns to his audience to ask whether they have any additional remarks to make.]

[Kravchenko (a brigadier) criticizes the foreman of another shop and a number of other workers. Some other workers criticize their foremen.]

Koliada: These people are working without a soul, without a soul, without fire. [He emphasizes the importance of the struggle for economy in the use of metal, fuel, instruments; criticizes the way in which chisels and pincers are thrown about. He then turns to a worker.] How many pincers did you throw out, Comrade Gusenkov?

Gusenkov (*master* of the pneumatic sledge hammer division): Many.

—And where are they?

—Everywhere.

—They have been thrown about everywhere.

—Let us take the chisels? How much does a chisel cost, Comrade Gusenkov?

Gusenkov: I didn't count.

Koliada: But for example, two, four, six rubles?

Gusenkov: No, more, ten rubles.

Koliada: Here, you see, ten rubles. And just imagine that while going around the shop you find ten-ruble notes thrown on the floor. Each one of you would undoubtedly lean down to pick them up. Why, then, are the chisels which are worth ten rubles lying around and nobody picks them up? Is it possible to have such an uneconomical attitude towards work? . . .

Savenkov: Will the administration of the shop and the administration [*upravlenie*] of the plant support the plan of repair or not?

Koliada: It is difficult for me to answer that question. I don't know what the administration plans to do. But I do know that the Ministry of Ferrous Metallurgy issued a directive to the effect that planned . . . preventive repairs be carried out firmly in correspondence with the ability of plant and shop.

Fedorov (another worker): [Starts out by saying that each worker will ponder about the significance of the example of the chisel.] Along with this, I want to say something about the disorders in our shop. . . . We still have a *master* who only realizes the production program quantitatively and not qualitatively, who doesn't think of economizing metals and materials. Machinery is neglected. Cranes will become worn soon, if things go on this way.

The prewar order must be restored. Until the war, the *master* was felt more in the shop as the boss of his division, and we, the workers, were consulted. I will ask as a worker: More discussions, more meetings must be held with us. Before the war, there were more meetings, more criticisms of one another and things went along more happily, inadequacies were repaired more quickly. . . .

Koliada: Comrade Federov, I agree that the role and accountability of the *rukovoditel* on his assigned division must be raised, but a single *master* and brigadier cannot do anything if he is not supported, if the workers do not aid him.

[A number of other people discuss ways to raise production.]

Koliada: Your remarks are correct. I have taken them down to give them to the foreman of the shop to take measures. There is no doubt that with the aid of the party organization of our shop which will study all these remarks, your proposals will be brought to life.

A Voice: These remarks should be shown to the director of a factory, Comrade Matevosian.

Koliada: Yes, I will do this. Secondly, as to instruments, pincers, chisels, etc., here much can be done without the intervention of the director of the factory, or of the foreman of the shop. And it must be done right away, without waiting for directives from above. Third, from all your remarks one thing is clear. The Five-Year Plan can be realized in the factory and in particular in our shop not only in four years, but even sooner. We will fight persistently for this. Fourthly, I will ask you to discuss what we have said here with all the members of your brigade, with all absent comrades, so as to mobilize them for the fulfillment of the Five-Year Plan in four years. . . . You must tell them in such a way as to speak from your heart how indispensable, how important for the people and the State is the fulfillment of the Five-Year Plan in four years. I am convinced that our glorious collective with new work advances will answer the appeal of those from Leningrad to fulfill the Five-Year Plan in four years.

APPENDIX G

"YOUR STRENGTH"[170]

(Poem about Atomic Energy)

You shuddered. The distant hollow rumble
Of your carriage
Sounded like a wind.
Sleep, my baby,
Your doll, your teddy bear and your little black devil are sleeping peacefully
   like children.
Where did that sudden jolt come from?
What does that signify?
In the Taiga, far away from here
In quite another end of the country,
Where the color of the yellow leaves
Does not glow away until spring.

There stands a granite mountain
Which is barring our way.
Long, long ago it should have been turned
Upside down
Long, long ago it should have been forced to give up its ore.
Sleep, my daughter,
The night is dark,
Sleep, my baby.
At that place there lived a group of geologists
In frost and heat.
Twelve months long
They were groveling around on the mountain.
Then there came an airplane full of professors to that place and then a platoon
   of army engineers,
First class lads,
And their young commander,

---

[170] Y. Dolmatovsky, "Tvoya Sila" ("Your Strength"), *Novyi Mir,* July, 1949, p. 170;
translation in *The New York Times,* September 25, 1949, used here with slight alteration.

And he was ordered to lay down an explosive shell.
It was not gunpowder, nor dynamite.

There is far more powerful stuff
Now in your country.
I will not tell its name.
Sleep, my baby.

At the pre-arranged hour, the explosion occurred.
The granite was blown asunder to dust.
The Taiga around the mountain was illuminated
By golden radiance.
The old mountain disappeared and the roar of the explosion interrupted at
  five in the morning
The sleep of children
As a breath of wind
From far, far away.

Sleep, little girl,
Your hand lies in my hand.
May the sound wave reach the foreign coasts
And warn our enemies
Who hear it there.
The mountain moldered away like flame and gave away its ore,
Not long ago only a fairy tale,
This has now occurred.
Sleep, my baby.

Index